Bricks and Mortarboards

A Report from EDUCATIONAL FACILITIES LABORATORIES, INC. on College Planning and Building.

Library of Congress Catalog Card No. 64-14232
Printed in U.S.A.
Second Printing, May, 1964

Single additional copies are available without cost
from Educational Facilities Laboratories, 477 Madison Avenue, New York 22, N. Y.

Acknowledgements

Max Abramovitz, Partner, Harrison & Abramovitz, Architects

Robert E. Alexander, Robert E. Alexander and Associates, Architects

Kenneth Anderson, consulting architect, University of California at La Jolla

William Anshen, Partner, Anshen & Allen, Architects

George F. Baughman, President, New College

Welton Becket, Welton Becket and Associates, Architects

Anthony A. Bernabei, Director, CIT Campus Homes Program

John C. Biardi, Provost, Long Island University

Donald V. Black, Director, Library Operations Survey, University of California at Los Angeles

W. Robert Bokelman, Chief, Business Administration Section, Division of Higher Education, U.S. Dept. of Health, Education and Welfare

Carl Borgmann, Director of the Program in Science and Engineering, Ford Foundation

Philip Brotherton, Partner, Perkins and Will, Architects

C. William Brubaker, Partner, Perkins and Will, Architects

Mary I. Bunting, President, Radcliffe College

Porter Butts, Editor of Publications, Association of College Unions, University of Wisconsin

Jack Campbell, Project Planner, John Carl Warnecke and Associates

C. Ray Carpenter, Director, Division of Academic Research and Services, Pennsylvania State University

William C. Caudill, Partner, Caudill, Rowlett & Scott, Architects

Victor Christ-Janer, Victor Christ-Janer & Associates, Architects

Verner Clapp, President, Council on Library Resources

James S. Coles, President, Bowdoin College

Sol Cornberg, President, Sol Cornberg Associates, Inc.

Walter Henry Costa, Skidmore, Owings & Merrill, Architects

James Dineen, International Business Machines Corporation

Richard P. Dober, Planning Faculty, Graduate School of Design, Harvard University

Jay du Von, Director, College Housing Branch, Housing and Home Finance Agency

Alden B. Dow, Alden B. Dow, Inc., Architects

Andrew Eaton, Librarian, Washington University

Anton J. Egner, Coordinator of Planning, Cornell University

Joseph C. Ekkers, Vice President, CIT Educational Housing Division

Ralph Ellsworth, Director of Libraries, University of Colorado

Donald P. Ely, Director, Audiovisual Center, Syracuse University

Russell N. Fairbanks, Assistant Dean, Columbia Law School

Philip W. Faulconer, consulting architect, University of California at La Jolla

John E. Forsberg, Director of Residences, Stanford University

Emery Foster, Director of Housing and Food Services, Michigan State University

John Guy Fowlkes, School of Education, University of Wisconsin

Arthur C. Frantzreb, Arthur C. Frantzreb and Co., Inc., Counsel for Institutional Planning and Financial Development

Morton Gassman, School of Architecture, Rensselaer Polytechnic Institute

Robert L. Geddes, Group for Planning and Research, Inc.

Noble Givden, Board of Cooperative Educational Services, Westchester County, N.Y.

King Graf, Vice President, Hellmuth, Obata & Kassabaum, Inc., Architects

Alan Green, School of Architecture, Rensselaer Polytechnic Institute

Tony Hall, Staff Member, Library, University of California at Los Angeles

James Hancock, Project Architect, Anshen & Allen, Architects

Harry Harmon, Chief, College Facilities Planning, California State Colleges

Robert Hayes, President, Advanced Information Systems Co.

Ray Hebert, Urban Plans Editor, *The Los Angeles Times*

Herman Henkle, Librarian, John Crerar Library, Chicago

Ernest V. Hollis, Director, College and University Administration, U. S. Dept. of Health, Education and Welfare

Robert Holz, Assistant Registrar, Massachusetts Institute of Technology

Henry James, Assistant Librarian, Lamont Undergraduate Library, Harvard University

John X. Jamrich, Assistant Dean, College of Education, Michigan State University

Roy Johnson, Director of Communication Services, University of Miami

Carl D. Johnson, Johnson, Johnson & Roy, Inc., Landscape Architects

William J. Johnson, Johnson, Johnson & Roy, Inc., Landscape Architects

Herbert J. Klausmeier, School of Education, University of Wisconsin

H. Peter Klein, Architect

Wayne Koppes, Architect

Ernest J. Kump, Kump Associates, Architects

Lawrence Lackey, Architect-Planner

Ralph C. Leyden, Director of Educational Development, Stephens College

Frank G. Lopez, Ballard Todd Associates, Architects

Charles Luckman, Charles Luckman Associates, Architects

Eugene Mackey, Partner, Murphy and Mackey, Architects

Charles Madden, former coordinator, Stephens College House Plan

Ellsworth Mason, Librarian, Colorado College

Carl C. McElvy, Sr., Architect

Thomas A. McGoey, Business Manager, Columbia University

Keyes D. Metcalf, Library Consultant

Ronald Moskowitz, Education Editor, *San Francisco Examiner*

Robert Munson, University of Miami, Coral Gables, Florida

Joseph Murphy, Partner, Murphy and Mackey, Architects

Albert Navez, Biology Department, Boston University

Walter Andrew Netsch, Jr., General Partner in Charge of Design, Skidmore, Owings & Merrill, Architects

Gyo Obata, President, Hellmuth, Obata & Kassabaum, Inc., Architects

Ralph Parker, Librarian, University of Missouri

Kermit C. Parsons, College of Architecture, Cornell University

William L. Pereira, William L. Pereira and Associates, Architects

George Pierce, The Office of George Pierce-Abel B. Pierce, Architects

Joseph D. Pigott, Director, Physical Planning, Case Institute of Technology

Suren Pilafian, Architect

Morton A. Rauh, Vice President, Antioch College

Harold C. Riker, Director of Housing, University of Florida

Millard G. Roberts, President, Parsons College

Frank B. Rogers, Director, National Library of Medicine

Clarence Roy, Johnson, Johnson & Roy, Inc., Landscape Architects

Harold Rubin, Director of Public Relations, Stephens College

George Vernon Russell, George Vernon Russell and Associates, Architects

Jerome M. Sachs, Dean, Teachers College North, Chicago

B. T. Schuerman, S.J., Treasurer, St. Louis University

Louis Schultheiss, Director, Technical Operations, Library, University of Illinois

C. E. Silling and Associates, Architects

Len Singer, Director of Learning Resources, Florida Atlantic University

Newell J. Smith, Director of Housing, University of Wisconsin

Robert Fitch Smith, Architect

Burgess Stanley, Laboratory Planning Consultant, A. B. Stanley Co.

Elwin Stevens, Director of Planning and Development, State University of New York

Whitney S. Stoddard, Chairman, Sub-Committee of Standing Committee to Implement Angevine Report, Williams College

Don R. Swanson, Manager, Synthetic Intelligence Department, Thompson Ramo Woolridge, Inc.

E. Howland Swift, Residence Halls Administrator, University of California

Herbert H. Swinburne, Partner, Nolen & Swinburne, Architects

Mortimer Taube, President, Documentation, Inc.

Harold Taubin, Director, University Planning Office, University of Pennsylvania

Colonel Walter M. Teasdale, Assistant to President for Planning, State University College at Albany

Adrian TerLouw, Educational Consultant, Eastman Kodak Co.

Elisabeth Kendall Thompson, Senior Editor (West), *Architectural Record*

Stanley Torkelson, Office of Edward Durell Stone, Architect

A. E. Vivell, Dean, U. S. Navy Postgraduate Engineering School

Paul Vonk, Dean, University College, University of Miami

T. S. Warburton, Associate Superintendent, Division of College and Adult Education, Los Angeles Board of Education

William Warren, Dean, Columbia University Law School

Arthur Weimer, Dean, School of Business, Indiana University

Harvey White, Department of Physics, University of California at Berkeley

Robert White, Teachers College North, Chicago

Hubert Wilke, Educational Director, Teleprompter Corporation

Kenneth Williams, President, Florida Atlantic University

William L. Wilson, Vice President, CIT Financial Corporation

Theodore Wofford, Murphy and Mackey, Architects

Colonel William T. Woodyard, Air Force Academy

Wilbur Wright, Department of Physics, Colorado College

Richard Yale, General Atomic Division, General Dynamics Corporation

S. B. Zisman, Planning Consultant

3

This book is for the people who make basic decisions affecting the future of American higher education — college trustees, corporation and foundation executives, lawmakers, and potential donors.

These decision-makers will determine whether the nation's colleges and universities can perform a near-miracle of expansion to accommodate the burgeoning college enrollment projected for the next 10 to 15 years.

The problem is a more complex one than sheer numbers and building capacity. The decision-maker has another concern: new procedures and new technology are reshaping the academic process. The space built today for higher education must be adaptable to these changes and, therefore, useful for many years to come.

For these reasons, BRICKS AND MORTARBOARDS deliberately is not presented in the technical language of the educator, the planner, the architect, or the builder. Rather, Educational Facilities Laboratories has asked five professional writers to bring together the best available information on what is happening in the four major types of campus building—the classroom, the laboratory, the library, and the dormitory—and in the design of the campus itself. To do so, the writers toured the United States to talk to the professionals, presenting their findings in the chapters of this book.

It is our hope that BRICKS AND MORTARBOARDS will help insure that an unprecedented national investment in facilities for higher education will produce buildings that serve rather than stifle higher education in the crucial years ahead.

Educational Facilities Laboratories

Foreword

American colleges and universities, which now enroll an estimated 4,118,000 degree-credit students, will have to accommodate more than 7,000,000 by 1970 and more than 8,500,000 by 1975. Therein, their crisis—and their opportunity.

Economist Peter F. Drucker has calculated that, to take care of all the additional students expected on the campus by 1975, the colleges will have to construct new facilities equal to twice all of the campus buildings erected since Harvard opened its doors in 1636. More specifically, the government predicts that $19 billion will have to be spent on college construction and campus development between now and 1972.

Immense as it is, the task is complicated by irresistible pressures on the colleges to change as fast as they grow. The nation is coming to recognize that education holds, in the long run, the key to our future as a people. We are asking the colleges to produce not only more, but better-prepared graduates, particularly in the fields where Cold War competition is most obvious. Meanwhile, the body of knowledge, most notably scientific knowledge, is multiplying at a dizzying rate. The colleges already are offering courses in subjects that were nonexistent 10 or 20 years ago.

And the student is changing. He is better prepared than his counterpart of a decade ago. In many cases, he arrives on campus with a year or more of college-level studies under his belt. The traditional freshman courses no longer suffice; this new student requires more demanding fare. He is likely to go on to graduate studies, creating an expansion problem at that level. More of his classmates are women, and the number of married students increases every year.

In the face of all this ferment and expansion, the colleges are handicapped by a growing shortage of qualified teachers. If quality is not to suffer, it follows that higher education will have to recruit more teachers and offer higher salaries to attract them. Even then it will have to make better use of whatever talent it can muster. The latter need has touched off a revolution in teaching methods. The revolution is not yet full blown, but its advance guard has infiltrated the instructional front on many campuses. Television, electronic language laboratories, teaching machines, automated lecture halls, already are to be found in some colleges. And more sophisticated developments are on the horizon.

The conclusion is inescapable: nothing is certain about the shape of college facilities except the probability that what happens in them today will not be happening in them in the same way a decade from now. The educational process is changing, and college buildings must be designed to change with it.

Will the colleges rise to the challenge? Will they be able to put up enough good new buildings at the right time and in the right places?

At the moment, the answer appears to be "no."

Certainly, much is being done. California is planning a new, $270 million phase in its expansion program for an already extensive system of public universities, state colleges, and two-year community colleges. At UCLA alone, $370 million will have been spent between 1949 and 1967. New York will spend $700 million to double the current enrollment of 53,000 in its State University system by 1970. It will establish four new university centers, convert its teachers colleges into larger, liberal arts institutions, create new community colleges, and expand other elements of the system. In Illinois, $195 million has been earmarked for university expansion, including the creation of entire new universities in Chicago and at Edwardsville. Other states, notably Florida and Texas, are following suit, but not all of them are proceeding at anything like the pace set by the big three.

The private colleges and universities, more limited in their sources of capital, are expanding in modest fashion. Developments in the town of Amherst, Massachusetts, offer a good indication of the trend. Amherst College, a privately supported, liberal arts institution for men, has decided to expand its enrollment from 1,028 to 1,200 in the next few years and stop there. On the other side of town, the sprawling, publicly supported University of Massachusetts, which already has an enrollment of 7,018, expects to have 20,000 by 1975. And it has set no ceiling on growth beyond that figure.

A substantial drop in the private institutions' share of total enrollments and therefore in their importance seems inevitable. A few new private institutions have been established or are in the offing. But none of them approach the scale of the new public institutions. New College, which is to open in 1964 in Sarasota, Florida, was founded on the premise that "superior private education is necessary for the preservation of our way of life." But according to current plans, the College's

Enrollment: Public vs. Private

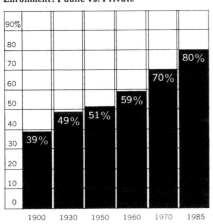

Publicly Sponsored Institutions	■	
Privately Sponsored Institutions	□	

enrollment never will exceed 2,400 students.

Despite all this activity, college and university expansion plans are falling short of the need, and actual construction is lagging behind the plans. The over-all gap between construction and needs is running at about $700 million a year. In other words, the colleges are spending about $1.2 billion a year on construction instead of the $1.9 billion the experts say is required.

The $1.9 billion estimate may be on the conservative side. It is based on the assumption that the colleges will be forced to make more efficient use of their facilities, improving the rate of utilization by about 20 per cent. This may be an optimistic viewpoint.

So far, the deficit appears to have had the primary effect of forestalling the replacement of obsolete facilities which may be inadequate for up-to-date instruction; poorly heated, lighted, or ventilated, unsafe, or all of these. But, if the deficit persists, the number of available seats in college classrooms will begin to fall short of the demand.

The root of the problem is money. The colleges are forced to allocate an inadequate supply among competing needs. Their reports to Washington indicate, for example, that they are taking money out of endowment and current income to pay for new buildings. And some of them have counted on the use of federal aid funds and commercial loans that have not been forthcoming.

Probably the stiffest competition for the college dollar is posed by the demand for higher faculty salaries. The faculty supply and demand picture has reversed itself in recent years. It has become a "professor's market" and salaries cannot be held at the low level, relative to the rest of the economy, that once was possible. They must be made competitive with those in industry.

The President's Committee on Education Beyond the High School, in a 1957 report, issued this warning:

"The plain fact is that the college teachers of the United States, through their inadequate salaries, are subsidizing the education of students, and in some cases the luxuries of their families, by an amount which is more than double the total of alumni gifts, corporate gifts, and endowment income of all colleges and universities combined. This is tantamount to the largest scholarship program in world history, but certainly not one calculated to advance education. Unless this condition is corrected forthwith, the quality of American higher education will decline. No student and no institution can hope to escape the consequences."

A start has been made toward an adequate salary structure, stimulated in part by the Ford Foundation's College Grants Program. The median salary for all faculty ranks was about $5,200 in 1955. By 1962, it had risen to $7,486, according to the National Education Association.

There is another, almost paradoxical drain on the colleges' resources in the proliferation of contract research on the campus. In 1940, $1 out of every $25 spent on higher education went to research. By 1960, the ratio had jumped to $1 out of every $5. And it is predicted that more than $1 out of every $3 spent on higher education in 1975 will go to research. Most of the increase has been in federally sponsored programs.

On one hand, the growth of these research programs has aided higher education. The level of research and adequacy of research facilities has been improved at many contracting institutions, helping them to attract better faculty and graduate students.

On the other hand, research activities have cut into the teaching load of many faculty members. Many research contracts, particularly

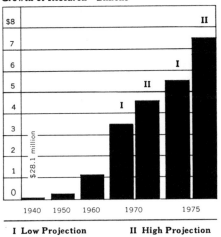

Growth of Research · Billions

$8 II
7
6 I
5 II
4 I
3
2 $28.1 million
1
0

1940 1950 1960 1970 1975

I Low Projection   II High Projection

those with the federal government, have not covered overhead costs in full. In some cases, construction funds for instructional buildings have been siphoned off for research facilities. And the fear has been expressed that the spread of these contractual relationships will make the universities a pawn of industry and government and undermine their primary function as educational institutions.

Finally, the colleges and universities are subject to the same inflationary pressures that affect the rest of the economy. Increases in all costs of higher education can be expected to continue. The higher education budget in 1970 is expected to more than triple the $3.6 billion spent in 1957-58. By 1975, the 1957-58 outlay will have multiplied more than five times.

But the experts hold that the nation can afford it. The top estimated budget for 1975, they point out, amounts to only 1.9 per cent of the projected gross national product for that year. The 1957-58 outlay represented .8 per cent of the GNP. The real question is how the added costs will be shared between students and parents; federal, state, and local governments; and private philanthropy.

It is argued that, because the student benefits monetarily from his college education, he ought to pay a larger share of the cost. Harvard economist Seymour E. Harris, for example, suggested that the following shifts in the financial burden might occur:[1]

	1957-58	1969-70
TUITION	25 PER CENT	40 PER CENT
GOVERNMENT	48 PER CENT	38 PER CENT
ENDOWMENT INCOME AND GIFTS	16 PER CENT	12 PER CENT
OTHER (SCHOLARSHIP FUNDS FROM VARIOUS SOURCES, ETC.)	11 PER CENT	11 PER CENT

Others, like Devereux C. Josephs, former Chairman of the Board of the New York Life Insurance Company, advocate that the student pay the full cost of his education. In an article published in 1959, he said:

"The solution to the problem is clear and simple: Colleges should raise tuition fees to charge to the student the full cost of his education, and what the student or his parents cannot pay from past savings and current earnings, they should borrow."

On the other hand, there are many who hold that our society benefits from the higher education of talented youth and that society ought to continue to pay its share of the cost and perhaps even increase its proportionate contribution.

Dr. John D. Millett, President of Miami University, Oxford, Ohio, is one who argues that no substantial changes should be made in the present methods of financing higher education. He questions the wisdom of widespread student borrowing, particularly borrowing by women. And he challenges the premise that would-be college professors should be charged the full cost of a Ph.D. or high school teachers the full cost of an M.A. In an article published several years ago, he said:

"Indeed, it is not clear that students should be encouraged to think of higher education only as a personal investment from which they should strive to obtain the greatest possible return. It is not clear that we want students channeled into high-salary professions rather than into important public service. It is not clear that we should adopt Russian methods of influencing individual behavior."[2]

Nevertheless, tuition is on the rise. And at least one institution, New College, has announced plans to charge its students the full cost of education when it opens in 1964. Dr. George F. Baughman, President of the College, estimated that tuition would exceed $2,000 a year.

There are differing viewpoints on the share of the load that will be carried by private philanthropy. The Council for Financial Aid to Education, which was established to encourage corporate giving to higher education, estimates that the gift and grant income of higher education in 1969-70 will cover 21 per cent of the total budget. Professor Harris finds the Council's outlook "very optimistic" and suggests that 12 per cent is a more realistic figure.

Some experts on philanthropy fear that increased state and federal contributions to higher education will tend to reverse the upward trend in private giving to the colleges and universities. Private donors, they point out, are likely to feel that the government is taking care of the colleges and, therefore, that private gifts are more needed elsewhere.

In fact, when Congressional approval of a broad federal aid program appeared imminent in 1962, some colleges postponed their campaigns for private gifts. They explained that they wanted to wait "until we find out what the federal government will do."

The experts note one trend that should be encouraging to colleges with expansion plans: private donors, corporations, and foundations have grown increasingly receptive to appeals for capital funds.

The colleges have found that 90 per cent of their income from private sources comes from only 10 per cent of the individuals solicited for funds. This, according to Arthur C. Frantzreb, fund-raising counsel, is due in part to the fact that, even though alumni gifts are increasing, "constant efforts to cajole alumni by every trick into more and greater gifts have failed to have a significant impact." The result has been a tendency to abandon large-scale, hard-hitting fund campaigns in favor of quiet solicitation among the "top 10 per cent," primarily personal foundations and wealthy individuals, and to seek more deferred giving through trust funds, annuities, and bequests.

The great unknown quantity is that of federal aid. There is no question that federal assistance to higher education has been with us a long time and that it will be increased. That much was made abundantly clear late in 1963, when the Congress authorized a $1.2 billion aid program to help the colleges and universities build classrooms, laboratories, and libraries.

But, at this writing, the Congress had only authorized the infusion of an average of $400 million a year for three years into the college construction kitty. The funds still had to be appropriated. And the new law did not come to grips with other areas of proposed federal assistance, such as scholarships for students.

Nevertheless, the measure heralded a massive increase in federal aid to the colleges and universities. Until its passage, Washington had been helping higher education to the tune of an estimated $500 million annually, not including research grants. It did so through loans for the construction of dormitories and other revenue-producing facilities, aid to land-grant colleges and universities, student loans and graduate fellowships under the National Defense Education Act of 1958, and fellowships and other projects supported by the National Science Foundation. The construction funds, then, represent an 80 per cent increase in Federal aid to higher education.

It must be stressed, however, that the new law does not solve the colleges' facilities problems. It does not even wipe out the apparent $700 million annual deficit in campus construction activity. And, most important, it makes no attempt to replace private support for college construction with federal funds.

To the contrary. The measure is intended to stimulate even more private gifts and loans for capital purposes to the colleges and universities. In most cases, colleges sharing in the $835 million authorized for grants must raise $2 from other sources for every $1 contributed by the government. (The exceptions are public community colleges and technical institutes. They must match the federal funds on a 60 per cent local/state and 40 per cent federal basis.) Applicants for $360 million in authorized 50-year, low interest loans, must put up at least one quarter of the total project cost.

Government experts predicted the $1.2 billion in federal aid would generate at least another $1.2 billion in new private gifts and loans for campus construction. It was pointed out that college projects now should be more attractive to the donor: with federal aid, he can buy $3 worth of building for $2.

The consensus of expert opinion is that there will be room on the American campus in 1970 and 1975 for every student who seriously desires education past the high school. But unless there is better planning by the educators and a greater financial commitment by society, there is danger that the needed facilities will be provided in a series of crash programs. Expediency rather than quality will be the byword. And our campuses will be crowded with misplaced academic slums, educationally self-defeating and a drain both educationally and economically on future generations.

J.J.M.

---

[1] Seymour Harris, "Higher Education: Resources and Finance" (New York: McGraw-Hill Book Company, Inc., 1962), p. 28.

[2] "Financing Higher Education:" 1960-70, ed. Dexter M. Keezer (New York: McGraw-Hill Book Company, Inc., 1962), p. 180.

CONTENTS

Money

The suggestion that as much as $19 billion will be needed in the next decade for campus development may smack of the extravagant. But the evidence, as compiled by Washington's practitioners of the inexact art of statistical prediction, is convincing. Their first, and most dramatic, assumption is underlined by the range of projected enrollments through 1975.

That the colleges are trying to meet the challenge is indicated by the funds they now are planning to spend on construction, how they plan to spend them, and where they expect the dollars to come from. But all this apparently is not enough as demonstrated by comparison between the estimated need, the colleges' plans, and their actual performance.

The problem is not one of facilities alone; the colleges need more money for all purposes. The total higher education budget in 1957-58 amounted to $3.6 billion. The economists predict drastic increases in the total budget but, projecting the gross national product, conclude that we can afford it.

Who is to pay the bill? Some hold that the student (or his parents) ought to pay a greater share if not the total cost of his higher education. Others passionately reject the idea. But all agree that the faculty cannot be made to continue to subsidize low tuition payments by accepting low salaries.

There are experts who maintain that private giving can fill the gap. But other, equally respected observers argue that, only by a vast increase in aid from all levels of government, can American higher education meet the challenge of the 1960's.

THE COLLEGE ENROLLMENT BOOM: 1950-1975

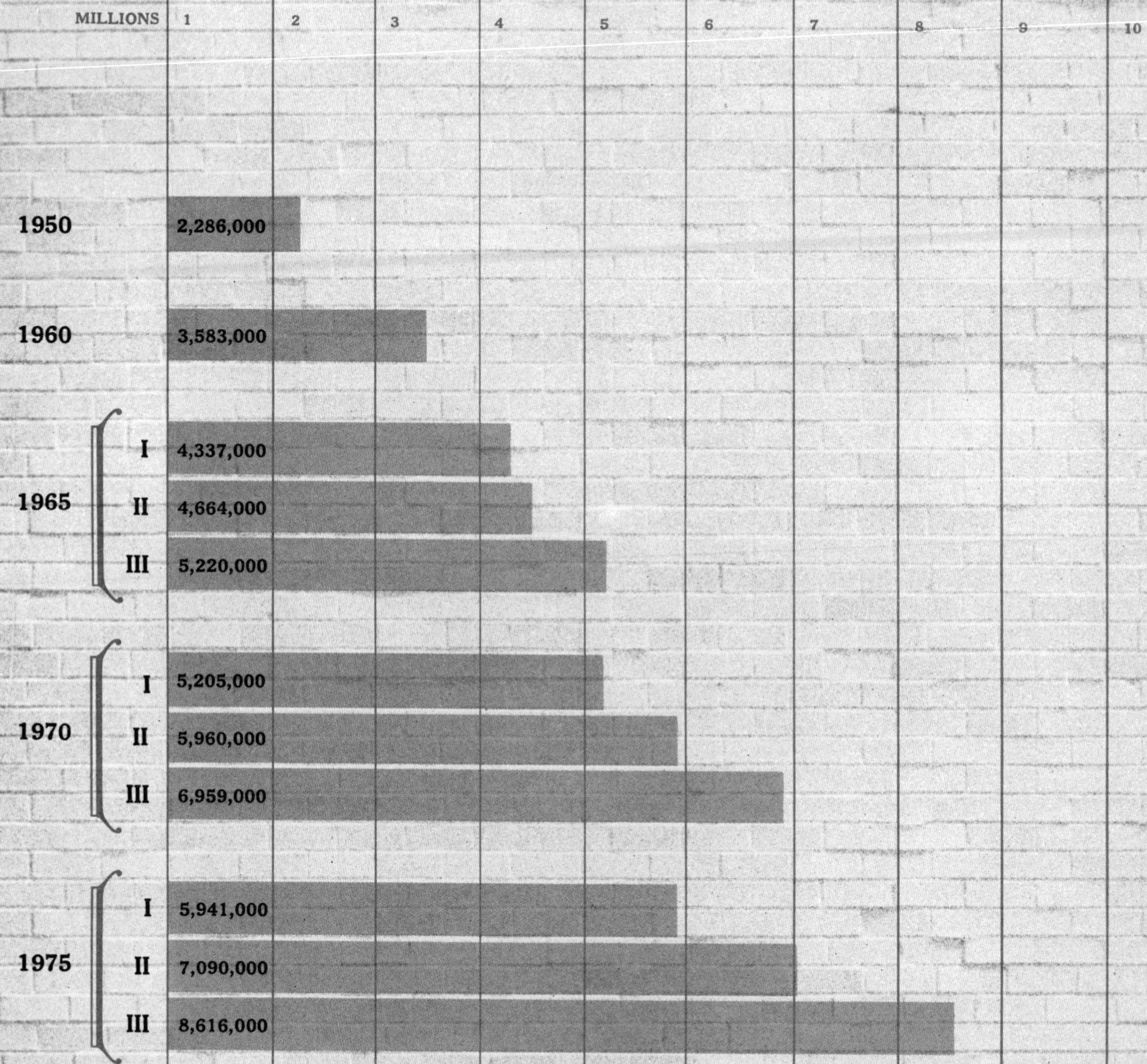

MILLIONS | 1 | 2 | 3 | 4 | 5 | 6 | 7 | 8 | 9 | 10

1950   2,286,000

1960   3,583,000

1965
- I   4,337,000
- II   4,664,000
- III   5,220,000

1970
- I   5,205,000
- II   5,960,000
- III   6,959,000

1975
- I   5,941,000
- II   7,090,000
- III   8,616,000

PROJECTIONS

I   Assumes rate of college attendance will be unchanged.

II   Assumes rate will increase, but only because of tendency of offspring of college-trained fathers to go to college.

III   Assumes current rate of increase will continue.

Source: ECONOMICS OF HIGHER EDUCATION, U.S. Office of Education, 1962.

WHAT THE COLLEGES ARE BUILDING 1961-'65   total: $7,524,590,000

Source: Dr. W. Robert Bokelman, U.S. Office of Education (percentages are rounded)

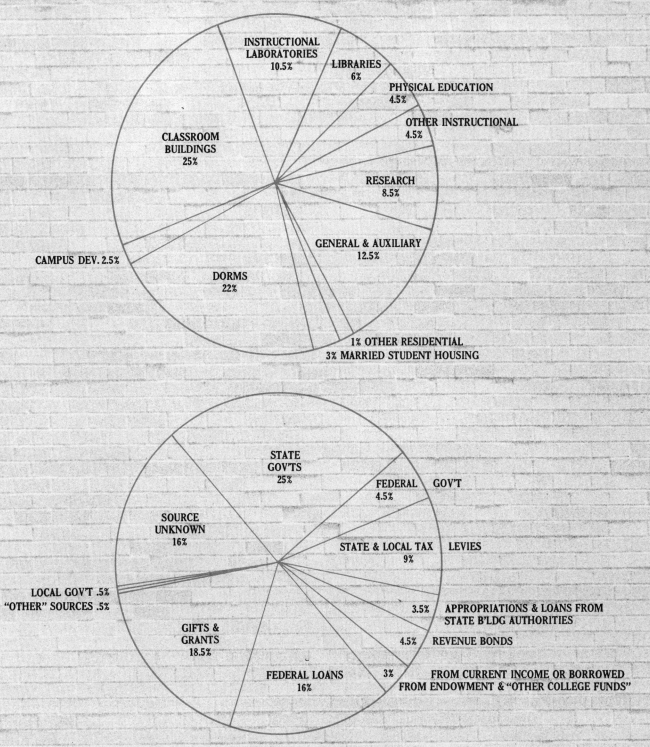

INSTRUCTIONAL
LABORATORIES
10.5%

LIBRARIES
6%

PHYSICAL EDUCATION
4.5%

OTHER INSTRUCTIONAL
4.5%

RESEARCH
8.5%

CLASSROOM
BUILDINGS
25%

GENERAL & AUXILIARY
12.5%

CAMPUS DEV. 2.5%

DORMS
22%

1% OTHER RESIDENTIAL
3% MARRIED STUDENT HOUSING

STATE
GOV'TS
25%

FEDERAL   GOV'T
4.5%

SOURCE
UNKNOWN
16%

STATE & LOCAL TAX   LEVIES
9%

LOCAL GOV'T .5%
"OTHER" SOURCES .5%

3.5%   APPROPRIATIONS & LOANS FROM
STATE B'LDG AUTHORITIES

4.5%   REVENUE BONDS

GIFTS &
GRANTS
18.5%

FEDERAL LOANS
16%

3%   FROM CURRENT INCOME OR BORROWED
FROM ENDOWMENT & "OTHER COLLEGE FUNDS"

WHERE THE MONEY IS COMING FROM   1961-'65   Source: U.S. Office of Education (percentages are rounded)

THE PROBLEM: THE COLLEGES ARE PLANNING FEWER NEW BUILDINGS THAN NEEDED AND ACTUAL CONSTRUCTION IS FALLING SHORT OF THE PLANS.

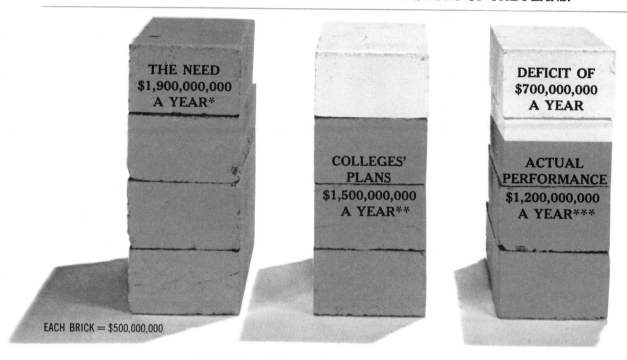

THE NEED
$1,900,000,000
A YEAR*

COLLEGES'
PLANS
$1,500,000,000
A YEAR**

DEFICIT OF
$700,000,000
A YEAR

ACTUAL
PERFORMANCE
$1,200,000,000
A YEAR***

EACH BRICK = $500,000,000

* U.S. Office of Education Estimates
** Colleges' Reports of Building Plans, 1961-65
*** Colleges' Plans Less Dollar Deficit Estimated by U.S. Office of Education

THE DEFICIT REPRESENTS:

A gap of $400 million a year between the colleges' plans for 1961-65 and the estimated need for the period of $9.5 billion.

A gap of $300 million between available construction funds and the colleges' plans. The causes:

More than $1.1 billion, or 15.4 per cent of the $7.5 billion the colleges planned to spend over the five-year period was listed as coming from "unknown" sources.

The colleges were counting on $308 million in Federal funds called for under aid to higher education programs that had not materialized.

The private colleges planned to borrow $200 million to build facilities that would not produce revenue. It was estimated that only $50 to $60 million would be forthcoming.

The colleges planned to spend $123 million out of current revenue and "borrow" $45 million from endowment and $49 million from "other college funds."

All this indicated that the colleges actually are spending only $5.9 billion over the five-year period and, if they stopped siphoning off funds intended for other uses, could spend only $5.7 billion. The deficit, then, ranges between $3.6 and $3.8 billion or, at the lower figure, $712 million a year.

WHERE HIGHER EDUCATION GETS ITS DOLLARS...

Source: Keezer, Dexter M., Editor, FINANCING HIGHER EDUCATION, 1960-70; New York, 1959, McGraw-Hill

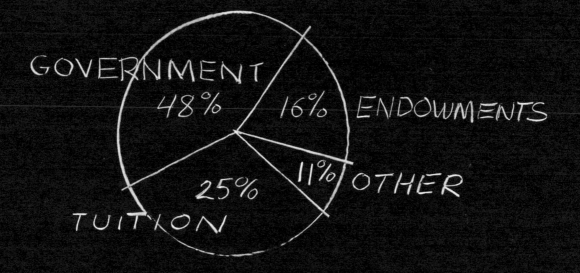

GOVERNMENT 48%

16% ENDOWMENTS

25% TUITION

11% OTHER

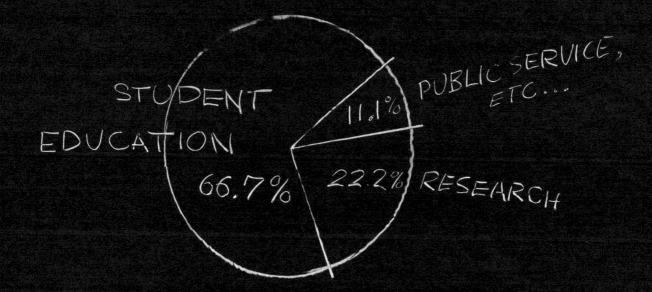

STUDENT EDUCATION 66.7%

11.1% PUBLIC SERVICE, ETC...

22.2% RESEARCH

...AND WHERE THEY ARE SPENT.

Source: ECONOMICS OF HIGHER EDUCATION, Washington, 1962, U.S. Office of Education

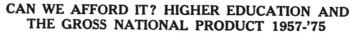

CAN WE AFFORD IT? HIGHER EDUCATION AND THE GROSS NATIONAL PRODUCT 1957-'75

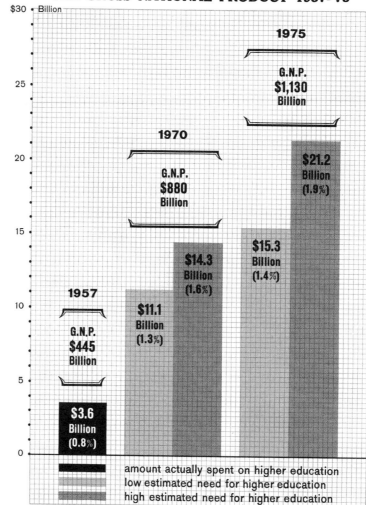

1975
G.N.P. $1,130 Billion
$21.2 Billion (1.9%)

1970
G.N.P. $880 Billion
$14.3 Billion (1.6%)
$15.3 Billion (1.4%)

$11.1 Billion (1.3%)

1957
G.N.P. $445 Billion
$3.6 Billion (0.8%)

amount actually spent on higher education
low estimated need for higher education
high estimated need for higher education

Source: Mushkin, Selma J., Editor, Economics of Higher Education, Washington, 1962, U.S. Government Printing Office

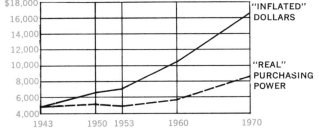

INCREASED FACULTY SALARIES: PROFESSOR (AVERAGE)

"INFLATED" DOLLARS

"REAL" PURCHASING POWER

$18,000
16,000
14,000
12,000
10,000
8,000
6,000
4,000

1943   1950 1953   1960   1970

Source: Tickton, Sidney G., NEEDED: A TEN YEAR COLLEGE BUDGET,
New York, 1961, The Fund for the Advancement of Education

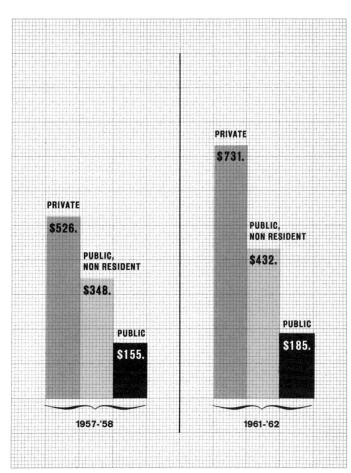

THE TUITION PICTURE:

AVERAGE TUITION AND REQUIRED FEES

PRIVATE
$731.

PUBLIC, NON RESIDENT
$432.

PUBLIC
$185.

PRIVATE
$526.

PUBLIC, NON RESIDENT
$348.

PUBLIC
$155.

1957-'58

1961-'62

Source: American Association of University Professors

The Council for Financial Aid to Education maintains that private gifts, from industry, individuals, and foundations, will continue to pay their share of the cost of higher education. Total voluntary support passed the $1 billion mark in 1960-61, according to CFAE estimates, and will reach $2 billion a year by 1969-70. This, the Council says, will be a reasonable share of the total budget if higher education operates at "utmost efficiency" and holds its 1969-70 outlay to $9 billion. The chart below indicates the trends in the amount and purposes of private giving to higher education as reported in four biennial surveys conducted by CFAE. (Survey responses represent an estimated 80 per cent of all private giving to higher education.)

Comparison of Purposes of Support: 1954-55, 1956-57, 1958-59 and 1960-61

(with percentage of Grand Total)

PURPOSES	1954-55	1956-57	1958-59	1960-61	GRAND TOTALS, FOUR SURVEYS
UNRESTRICTED	$ 82,456,728	$180,364,047	$191,213,039	$218,512,356	$672,546,170
	28.6%	24.5%	30.5%	27.2%	27.4%
PHYSICAL PLANT	66,481,431	139,774,200	160,396,143	215,534,618	582,186,392
	23.0%	18.9%	25.6%	26.8%	23.7%
FACULTY COMPENSATION	21,470,718	219,191,597	44,995,787	44,352,024	330,010,126
	7.4%	29.7%	7.2%	5.5%	13.4%
BASIC RESEARCH	36,267,510	72,733,866	87,368,988	1,12,976,530	309,346,894
	12.5%	9.9%	14.0%	14.1%	12.6%
STUDENT FINANCIAL AID	35,604,446	56,317,272	82,887,173	96,124,102	270,932,993
	12.2%	7.6%	13.2%	12.0%	11.0%
OTHER PURPOSES	47,260,687	69,737,123	59,722,432	115,485,966	292,206,208
	16.3%	9.4%	9.5%	14.4%	11.9%
TOTALS	$289,541,520	$738,118,105	$626,583,562	$802,985,596	$2,457,228,783

Source: VOLUNTARY SUPPORT OF AMERICA'S COLLEGES AND UNIVERSITIES: 1960-1961
New York: Council for Financial Aid to Education, 1962, p. 14

CLASSROOMS

CLASSROOMS
by
Mel Elfin

A major new university is rising from the rubble of a massive slum clearance project on Chicago's South Side. There, at the intersection of two of the nation's busiest expressways, the University of Illinois is building a new, $150 million city campus. The new university, scheduled to open sometime in 1964, eventually will be the academic home for 20,000 students. And it may become an architectural prototype for urban universities of the future. Its significance as a model is symbolized by a "Great Court" that will be at the heart of the tight, 106-acre metropolitan campus.

The court, like the agoras of ancient Greece and the piazzas of Renaissance Italy, will serve as a great public square for the University's commu-

nity of scholars. Set one story above ground and free of vehicular traffic, the court will become a center of busy, bustling human traffic. With its four huge exedras (circular concrete benches) and 2,500-seat Greek amphitheater, the court also will be a natural meeting and resting place for students and faculty. As architect Walter A. Netsch, Jr., of the Chicago office of Skidmore, Owings and Merrill, put it:

"It should be a perfect spot for student rallies, for jam sessions, for meeting dates, and for just sitting in the sun and feeling young—or at least trying to."

The court represents an imaginative attempt at creating a feeling of community on a big city campus. How-

ever, its most significant feature is not what will take place on it, but under it. Actually, the court is something of an illusion: in reality it is the paved and landscaped roof of a one-story lecture center.

With 20,000 students on its rolls, the new campus will require an assortment of facilities for large-scale instruction. Rather than scattering these facilities across the campus, architect Netsch has grouped them in a single building. The resulting plan calls for a lecture center including nine auditoriums seating 250 students; six seating 75; three seating 150; one seating 500; and two, 250-seat halls equipped for scientific and other "wet" demonstrations.

The need for such a variety of large-scale teaching spaces for a single university illustrates one of the paramount problems troubling college authorities everywhere: the campus is becoming crowded with more and more students. Unhappily, the supply of teachers is not growing as fast as the supply of students. This means that the college professor of tomorrow will have to teach and reach far more students than his colleague of today. New campus facilities like the Chicago lecture center must therefore be designed to help the professor instruct large groups of students as efficiently as possible.

At the same time, tomorrow's professor will have to cover more ground in the same period of time. The body of knowledge is expanding even faster than the body of students. Clearly, if

Lecture Center, University of Illinois, Chicago

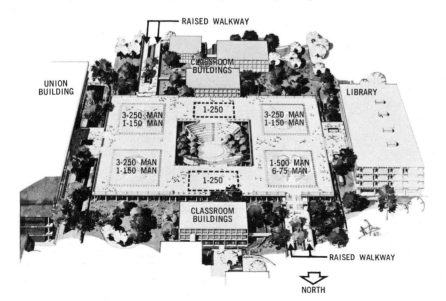

RAISED WALKWAY

UNION
BUILDING

CLASSROOM
BUILDINGS

LIBRARY

3-250 MAN
1-150 MAN

1-250

3-250 MAN
1-150 MAN

3-250 MAN
1-150 MAN

1-500 MAN
6-75 MAN

1-250

CLASSROOM
BUILDINGS

RAISED WALKWAY

NORTH

coming generations of college students are to keep pace with a world of accelerating change, the learning process itself will have to undergo accelerating change.

Fortunately, modern technology offers higher education a deskful of valuable aids with which, hopefully, it can promote more efficient instruction. Films, television, tape recorders, slide projectors, computers, and test-scoring machines are all tools both teacher and student may employ to cope with the educational demands of the future. The significant fact is not that this equipment exists, but that hitherto it has been so little used by institutions probing the frontiers of human knowledge. Hubert Wilke, educational director of the Teleprompter Corporation (which was a pioneer in the application of technology to pedagogy) said: "Almost every field of human endeavor is assisted by the tools of modern technology. There is no reason why the teaching profession should not be so assisted."

PROBING INNER SPACE

What do all these changes and potential changes mean for the college planning new instructional facilities?

For one thing, new classroom buildings and lecture halls must enable a relatively smaller number of teachers to instruct a relatively larger number of students. This can be achieved only in large teaching areas or in small areas which are linked electronically. On the other hand, new classroom buildings must also accommodate and encourage independent study as students are thrown more and more on their own. This requires an entirely different kind of space, one emphasizing privacy and individuality. And the campus also must include spaces for the traditional, and invaluable, small group and seminar instruction.

Some colleges, of course, are big enough or affluent enough to afford a variety of spaces for a variety of educational purposes. However, since most institutions operate on severely limited budgets, they frequently must make the same spaces do double and even triple duty. Their new classroom buildings must be designed to be both flexible in size and adaptable in function. A college may have no immediate plans for using any of the new electronic classroom aids. Nevertheless, new buildings should be designed to allow for their possible introduction later on without great additional expense. Thus, the necessary cables, electrical outlets, and utilities should be installed when a building is constructed, not after it is open and in operation. As architectural afterthoughts, electronic aids can be prohibitively expensive.

Walter Netsch was very much aware of the problems of technological obsolescence when he designed the University of Illinois campus in Chicago. All the major instructional areas on the

campus, including six low-rise classroom buildings, will be equipped with conduits and cables that will permit the institution to keep up with future electronic developments. Mr. Netsch also hedged his technological bets in planning the audio-visual facilities in the lecture center. He has designed several auditoriums for both front and rear projection (to be discussed at length later on). "These buildings," says the architect, "represent the best gamble we could make, considering that educational technology is not a fixed art."

The Chicago plan also represents, in the most concrete fashion, a burgeoning trend in campus design—the grouping of spaces according to function rather than academic discipline. On more and more campuses, chemistry and physics buildings are emerging as laboratory and science centers. History and mathematics buildings are giving way to unlabeled classroom and lecture centers. For example, no fewer than 10 lecture centers similar to the one at Chicago are on the drawing boards or under construction at various units of the widely scattered State University of New York. The centers, based on a design concept developed by Morton C. Gassman and Alan C. Green, two bright young members of the School of Architecture faculty at Rensselaer Polytechnic Institute, vary greatly in size.

On some of the smaller campuses, the centers will include as few as eight auditoriums ranging in size from 40 to

120 seats. In contrast, the elegant campus planned for the new State University Center at Albany by Edward Durell Stone, will boast one huge building housing 20 auditoriums, ranging all the way from six double classrooms seating 60 each to a theater-sized hall seating 500 students. As at Chicago, the New York lecture centers will lie at the physical as well as the pedagogical heart of their respective campuses.

"We've probably gone overboard on providing large spaces, particularly at Albany," said Elwin Stevens, director of planning and development for the State University. "However, at the rate with which our enrollments are increasing, there is a good possibility that our projections for the future may be too low. If that happens, the facilities for large group instruction may be even more important."

With a larger proportion of the student's time devoted to lectures, the seminar room and study desk will assume a new and critical importance. If the material offered in the lecture hall is to be explained, amplified, and questioned — if real teaching, rather than the simple transmission of facts, is to occur — maximum effectiveness must be built into seminar rooms, classrooms, and individual study facilities.

The new, $2.75 million James W. Wood Learning Center at Stephens College in Columbia, Missouri, reflects an awareness of that need. The red brick and glass complex, now under construction, houses a 300-seat teach-

ing auditorium, a 135-seat theater-lecture hall, and an assortment of classrooms seating between 25 and 80 students. But the center, built at a cost of about $22 per square foot, also includes 67 faculty offices, each one planned to do double duty as a small seminar room seating six to eight students.

Behind the plan is the intent to maintain a long-cherished tradition, shared by Stephens (enrollment: less than 1,800) with many institutions of similar size — informality and close student-faculty relations. The office-seminar spaces offer not only an economy, but the opportunity for frequent, direct contact between teachers and students.

A comparable experiment will be tried at the new university to be opened by the State of Florida in Boca Raton, on its southeast coast. Called Florida Atlantic University, the new institution will be the first, if not the only, university in the nation dedicated solely to the junior and senior years and graduate level education.

"This," says Dr. Kenneth Williams, president of the university-to-be, "means that we will have more mature students who will be more highly motivated and know considerably more about the direction in which they are headed than the average student at other institutions. Consequently, our facilities will have to promote a greater intimacy between the student and the instructor, a feature of graduate education at most universities, and one that we will now have to bring down

to the undergraduate level." To accomplish this, Florida Atlantic plans to put faculty and students in close proximity.

The university will create something new in academic facilities—offices for commuting students. The student offices will be adjacent to faculty offices, a location the administration hopes will foster friendly, two-way traffic. The solution was arrived at partly because of the relative maturity of the prospective student body and partly because two-thirds of the students (estimated 1970 enrollment: 10,000) are expected to be commuters drawn from the sprawling megalopolis on Florida's southeast coastal strip. The student offices will be comparable to resident students' dormitory rooms in every respect, except that bed, bureau, and other appurtenances of living will not be included. But the offices, to be rented by the commuter on a semester-to-semester basis, will be convertible into dormitory space (and vice versa), should there be a change in the commuter-resident "mix."

The growing importance of the commuting student on the American campus is equally evident at Chicago Teachers College-North, a two-year-old institution operated by the Chicago Board of Education on a 33-acre, parklike site on Chicago's North Side. Architect Philip Brotherton of Perkins and Will has designed a cluster of buildings which is handsome, functional, and suited to the needs of a small (fewer than 2,000 students)

urban college devoted to training its commuting students as teachers.

For about $5.6 million, Chicago has acquired a 256,000-square-foot complex, including lecture halls seating 253 and 673 students, large classrooms for as many as 90 students, smaller spaces for seminar groups of up to 15 students, and spaces for individual and semi-individual study. The private study areas have been almost a Perkins and Will trademark since partners C. William Brubaker and Larry Perkins invented the term "Q (for Quest) Space" to describe their function. Others refer to them as student study stations or as carrels (after an ancient French word for a monk's cell). Two hundred of these Q-Spaces or carrels line the window-walls of several wide corridors at the college. The carrels, furnished with lockers, lamps, chairs, and formica-topped desks, cost about $175 each. Unfortunately, they have so far been the scene of far less questing than the Teachers College administration had anticipated.

One Midwest architect attributed their low utilization to the carrels' location. "Who wants to study in a corridor?" he asked. In reply, designer Brotherton insisted that the academic and extracurricular programs should be so planned that the Q-Spaces would become natural and regular study centers. However, one pretty young sophomore questioned the whole idea. "This is a commuters' college," she explained, "and no matter how interesting the after-school program and no matter how comfortable the facilities, it's usually easier to study at home. Besides, many of the girls are married or have boy friends, and they don't want to hang around school a moment longer than necessary. So when their classes are through, they go home."

THE WANDERING WALLS

The college's administrators are confident that, through time and changes in the educational program, the individual study areas ultimately will be fully utilized, commuting students or not. Meanwhile, the college has been much more successful in obtaining a high rate of utilization in other instructional areas. Its buildings, which cost about $19 a square foot to construct, receive the intensive use called for in an urban institution, where the high cost of land and construction must be taken into account. The secret: flexibility.

Each of the college's 13 instructional areas, for example, can be subdivided into smaller areas by means of immediately movable, operable walls. The operable wall is hardly new. Sliding, folding, or accordion-type partitions have been with us for many years. What is new about the new operable wall is its effectiveness as a sound barrier. The old operable partition was about as soundproof as a sieve. But the push-button models installed at Teachers College lack that acoustical disadvantage. Noise transmission between class areas has been reduced to the

point that activities in one room rarely distract classes on the other side of the partition. The architects had to go a step further, however, in solving the problem of noise from motion-picture sound tracks, normally not contained even by the most efficient operable partition. The solution was to replace the single loudspeaker normally used to cover an entire class area with a series of low-volume speakers mounted in the ceiling.

The operable walls at Teachers College cost about $52,000, or roughly five times the cost of permanent walls. But their installation has made possible an increase in the utilization rate of classroom space from an estimated 65 per cent to about 85 per cent. "As it works out in practice," Mr. Brotherton said, "the operable walls give Teachers College the equivalent of six additional classrooms." At the going rate for construction in Chicago, that is an unqualified bargain.

Columbia University has had equal success with the operable walls built into its new Law School on Morningside Heights in New York City. One of these walls, 15 inches thick and 17½ feet tall, divides a classroom seating 380 into two rooms seating 190 each. The same versatility was designed into the Law School's moot courtroom by architect Max Abramovitz of Harrison and Abramovitz. When the courtroom is not needed for the dispensation of mock justice, an operable wall slides in front of the judge's bench and witness chair and, *ipso facto*, the Law School

has another useful classroom.

Justifiably or not, the acoustics at Mr. Abramovitz's newest Manhattan project—Lincoln Center's Philharmonic Hall—have been subjected to noisy criticism. But no similar complaints have been voiced about Columbia's Law School. "The acoustics are so good," says Professor Jack Weinstein, "that even with a large class of more than 100 you can conduct a Socratic discussion in a conversational voice and have everyone in the room hear what's going on." The sliding walls are no problem to the teachers or students.

They are, however, a problem to the Columbia maintenance staff, which has complained that the panels take too long to move into place and that they frequently slide off their tracks. The staff also has reported that it takes more time (and therefore more money) to keep the nine-story Law School neat and clean than other campus buildings. The building, incidentally, cost more than $8 million, or between $26 and $27 per square foot, including air conditioning.

The operable wall is not the only means of producing convertible space on the campus. Consider the extraordinarily versatile area that architects Joseph D. Murphy and Eugene Mackey of St. Louis have designed for the Wood Learning Center at Stephens. Seating arrangements and lighting (and an operable wall), give the center a chameleon-like capacity for change: it can serve as an auditorium seating 150; as two 60-seat classrooms; as a small theater-in-the-round; or as an actor's lounge and rehearsal room for another theater down the corridor. Stephens also regards the lobby outside its 300-seat teaching auditorium, which doubles as an art exhibition hall, and the landscaping outside the learning center, used as a "living botanical library," as learning facilities.

Convertibility, flexibility, and versatility probably have been carried to their ultimate in higher education in the twin "concourses" at Delta College, a two-year-old institution in Saginaw, Michigan. To the startled outsider, the concourses may seem about as conducive to learning as a busy corridor in the Pentagon. But, Delta officials insist, "it works."

Set on the east and west sides of a glassed-in interior court, the 265 x 28-foot concourses function as walkways, lecture halls, art display halls, lounges, and small seminar areas. Fully carpeted (cost: $21,000), these combination classroom-corridors can simultaneously house groups of students clustered around one or more of 18 closed-circuit television monitors; groups of students relaxing on sofas or settees; or scattered individuals strolling through to the cafeteria. "It may sound confused in theory," says Franklin Bouwsma, assistant to the president of Delta, "but in practice there's no problem."

FUNCTION VS. DISCIPLINE

Delta College (principally designed by Alden Dow of Midland, Michigan)

Concourse at Delta College is a place to learn.

is an excellent example of the movement away from monumentality in the design of college campuses. Built as a simple, one-story rectangle, Delta bears little resemblance to the structures which have traditionally dominated the American campus. Architect Charles Brubaker of Perkins and Will explains that, through the nineteenth and most of the twentieth centuries, universities erected rigid, single-function buildings which were as unchanging and unchangeable as Greek temples. "These were buildings," observes Mr. Brubaker, "that seemed to say to the individual: 'You are nothing; the organization is what matters.'"

On the contemporary campus, Mr. Brubaker senses that rigidity and monumentality are yielding to a new concept of free-flowing space, an architecture that does not seek to dwarf the

individual but to serve him. Except in rare cases, such as a military institution like the Air Force Academy, Mr. Brubaker believes that monumentality is as out of place on the campus as a quarterback at the University of Chicago.

Walter Netsch, who designed the Air Force Academy, does not completely agree with Mr. Brubaker. He earnestly holds that too much flexibility and too many functions can rob a space of character. "There are many environmental advantages to committed space," says Mr. Netsch. "The feeling of permanence is just one. I myself would not like to go to school in a world in which everything might disappear the next day."

At the University of Illinois Chicago campus, Mr. Netsch shunned large-scale convertibility, but managed to commit his space gracefully. He was able to do so largely because of the sheer size of the institution. With 20,000 students and a construction budget of $150 million, Mr. Netsch could program any number of different sizes and kinds of lecture halls, classrooms, laboratories, and offices. Smaller and less affluent universities lack the advantage of size and may have to resort to operable walls and convertibility.

Is there a middle ground between Mr. Netsch's committed and Mr. Brubaker's convertible space?

Architect Gyo Obata of the St. Louis firm of Hellmuth, Obata and Kassabaum seems to have found that middle ground in his shrewd design for the

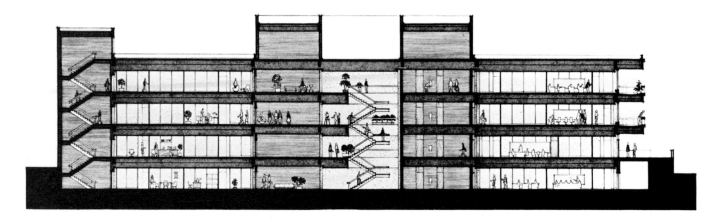

Two views of classroom building planned for Southern Illinois University at Edwardsville.
Service towers (shaded above, in black below) free instructional floor area for change.

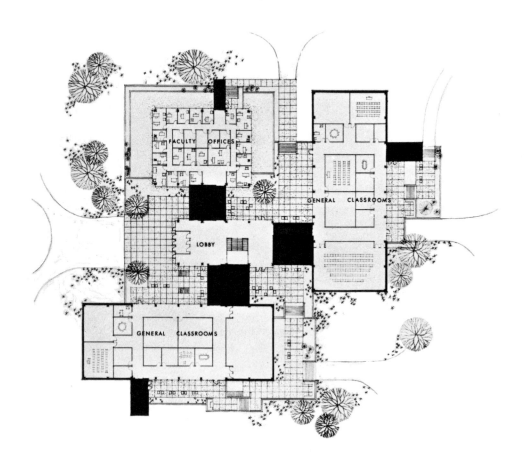

new branch of Southern Illinois University at Edwardsville. Mr. Obata found that there would be few occasions when instantaneous convertibility of space would be required. But some flexibility might be required on a campus scheduled to grow from 5,000 students in 1964 to 20,000 by 1970. To Mr. Obata this meant a requirement for change measured not in seconds or minutes, but in days and weeks. What he had in mind was the sort of alteration that might be accomplished between semesters or during school vacations. His solution was a design that keeps the main instructional areas free of any permanently fixed elements that might hinder the taking down and putting up of semi-permanent—or movable—partitions.

In his highly functional plan for the first classroom structures at Edwardsville, Mr. Obata has placed all the service elements—plumbing, stairs, elevators, etc.—in separate towers on the periphery of each building. Thus the entire 40 x 60-foot interior span of the buildings can be divided and re-divided as required. If desired, whole floor areas can serve as single large spaces; or, as most often will be the case, the areas can be partitioned off into classrooms seating 12, 24, 48, or 72 students.

Light, heat, air conditioning, and cables for closed-circuit television are brought into the individual classrooms through a three-foot dropped ceiling (the gross floor to ceiling height: 12 feet). At five-foot intervals, Mr. Obata has provided aluminum "T's" to facil-itate the erection of movable, sound-proof partitions. Each classroom will have its own movable chalkboards and tackboards. The architect estimates that the concrete, brick, and glass classroom buildings will cost about $23 to $24 per square foot. "Of course," says Mr. Obata, "the flexibility we have designed costs more, but the difference is not that great. In the long run, the flexibility will more than pay for itself."

A similar solution was reached by Mr. Brubaker in his design for Southern Illinois' new science and technology center on the main campus at Carbondale. He has planned a series of buildings connected by service towers. Given the continually changing nature of science teaching and research, it was necessary to provide as much interior flexibility as possible. The answer was to construct buildings in an architectural "chain" that permits expansion in any direction, with the service towers as connecting links. As Mr. Brubaker put it: "The plans allow the center to grow in a natural, agreeable manner and at a minimum of expense."

THE SHAPE OF EDUCATION

The debate over committed versus convertible space reflects a lively architectural interest in the design of the classroom itself. Unfortunately, there has been far less concern over what to put inside the classroom once it has been designed. Of the existing studies on the subject, one of the most useful and extensive was put together in 1961 by R. P. I.'s Morton Gassman, Alan Green, Harold Hauf, and Wayne F. Koppes. The study, called *New Spaces for Learning*, had one major shortcoming: most of the design principles were based on theory, not practice.

It was to test the principles outlined in *New Spaces* that the R. P. I. team constructed and furnished an experimental classroom on the Troy campus (aided, as in the case of the original study, by an EFL grant). The classroom mock-up is located in one of the newest and most unusual spaces for learning on any American campus—the crossing of a deconsecrated Roman Catholic Church.

The classroom-in-a-church is shaped, lighted, painted, and furnished in accordance with the tenets of *New Spaces*. The 100-student facility is equipped with several chalk and tackboards; a complete panoply of audio-visual projection equipment; raised seating and instruction platforms; continuous formica writing surfaces instead of individual desks; and an excellent sound system. The acoustics, in fact, proved to be a little too good. "When the classroom first opened," recalls Morton Gassman, "the sound of shuffling papers could be heard so clearly that we built a little acoustical 'perfume' (ambient sound) into the air-conditioning system to correct the condition."

In addition to a course in architectural history, the experimental classroom has been used for classes in economics, engineering, biology, and for a summer refresher course for high school science teachers. A poll of these teachers is to date the only significant attempt at evaluating the effectiveness of the classroom and its furnishings. The complaints were minor. For example, there was some criticism that the white writing surfaces were too "glary." Other teachers recommended that the edge of the surface be beveled, since it cut into their arms. But the over-all environment delighted most of the respondents. The reaction was summed up by one teacher, who wrote: "I wish I had one to teach in, in my school back home."

On a much more limited scale, Indiana University is experimenting with a new space for learning in the design for its new $5 million School of Business. Indiana plans what it calls the "10 by 10 classroom," in which swivel seats are arranged in 10 rows of 10 chairs each. This will permit the future executives to swivel through 360 degrees to view the chalkboards, tackboards, and projection screens arrayed along three walls of the classroom, as well as to follow the instructor and his assistant as they move around a three-sided platform. Students will be almost completely surrounded by learning stimuli, a situation that prompted Dean Arthur Weimer to remark facetiously: "It will be awfully hard for a kid to go to sleep in this classroom."

Wakefulness probably will be a by-product of another innovation being tried in the teaching auditorium of the University of Texas' new, $4.75 million academic center. Three stages and screens will be set in the shape of a "U" at the front of the lecture hall. The eyes of Texas students thus will be confronted by a variety of images. The students will have a choice among three varieties of seating: 116 fixed seats on a raised platform in the rear, 110 swivel chairs in the center, and 58 movable chairs in the front section.

Other features: microphones will be placed at every tenth seat to facilitate student discussion, and audio outlets for simultaneous translations will be installed at every chair. The translation capability will make it possible for the university to call upon many of the Spanish-speaking scholars who live in or visit Austin. The University of Miami, located in the center of a growing Spanish-speaking population, plans a similar installation.

Versatility of another sort is planned for a new Physical Sciences Lecture Hall at the University of California at Berkeley. The $600,000 hall will boast a revolving stage, the purpose of which will be educational, not theatrical. The design concept was explained in the April, 1960, issue of the *American Journal of Physics* by Berkeley's Professor Harvey White. Professor White proposed that the center section of the front wall of the auditorium — the chalkboards, and most of the long demonstration table and lecture platform—be built in triplicate. The three platforms would be arranged to form a triangle and then mounted on a large revolving platform. Utilities, such as electricity, gas, and compressed air needed for scientific purposes, would be brought in from a ring mounted above the center of the platform. Waste would be removed from below.

Thus, while one demonstration table and set of chalkboards were in use, laboratory assistants behind the scenes would be setting up physics and chemistry demonstrations for classes to follow. "Between periods," wrote Dr. White, "the push of a button will bring either of the prepared lecture fronts into the lecture room."

The White scheme attacks one of the major obstacles to better utilization of science teaching facilities—the great length of time normally required to set up classroom experiments. Sometimes a large lecture hall must remain empty for at least one period while apparatus from the previous class is removed and a new demonstration prepared. Even when only a few minutes are involved, they usually are subtracted from instructional time at the beginning of a class. Dr. White points out that some schools use roll-in demonstration tables, but that the very act of rolling-in consumes classroom time. Furthermore, the portable tables limit the size and type of demonstration apparatus which can be used. Professors sometimes prefer to skip an experiment rather than perform it with inadequate apparatus. The revolving stage is one answer.

Another answer, discovered by Professor White when he taught physics on a network television series, involves the problem of sight. No matter how efficiently a classroom experiment is handled, it is of little use to the student unless he can see it. To the student, an experiment in physics sometimes seems more like an exercise in eyestrain, particularly if he is at the rear of a large lecture hall. Some instructors have tried to overcome this deficiency by using oversized apparatus. But there is a point where giant equipment becomes more trouble than it is worth. And, some demonstrations simply cannot be enlarged. Professor White's solution: the television camera.

In his *American Journal of Physics* article, Professor White suggested that two or three television cameras be mounted above the demonstration tables to pick up the experiments. The images then would be transmitted on a closed circuit to monitors suspended from the ceiling of the auditorium. Even those students in the rear of the auditorium would have a close-up view of the demonstrations. Dr. White listed other advantages to the use of closed-circuit television in the lecture hall:

"Because television cameras can move in for close-up views, apparatus can be physically small. This means that most new devices are less expensive to make, require far less space for storage and are easily and quickly transported and set up in the lecture room.... Since the camera is focused on the exact area to be viewed, the students see exactly what the instructor wants them to see. As a result, the students are not distracted by things of little consequence."

Professor White's article focused attention on the second great change affecting the design of classroom buildings on the nation's campuses: the electronic revolution. Television, the motion-picture projector, the tape recorder, and similar devices are an old and by now familiar story on the campus. But until recently, television and the other audio-visual gadgetry have been used largely as occasional supplements for learning. Only in rare instances has a college or university harnessed the full pedagogical potential of the electron tube.

Now, however, a number of institutions have found that modern technology offers teaching aids of incalculable value. The result is that some architects are designing buildings as electronic machines as well as human shelter. In these cases, television, movie projectors, and the like no longer are installed in campus buildings as an afterthought. In a sense, the buildings are being designed around the machines, as was the case at the revolutionary University College at the University of Miami.

Opened in 1961, University College was conceived, designed, and engineered for the primary purpose of instructing large groups of students through the medium of closed-circuit television. Six of the eight pie-shaped wedges which make up the octagonal building are air-conditioned, windowless, 300-seat lecture halls. The other wedges are temporarily broken up into small classrooms. In the front of each lecture hall looms a 10-foot square viewing screen. Through these screens, televised instruction in the humanities and natural and social sciences is projected to most of Miami's 4,500 freshmen and sophomores. The televised lectures are supplemented by seminars and laboratories, but the video tube remains the sparkplug of underclass education on the Coral Gables campus.

The Miami octagon, which cost about $672,000—or $15.26 per square foot, including air conditioning—is a model of educational efficiency. In it, the University's finest lecturers sit in a television studio and address 1,800 students simultaneously. With the aid of video tape these same professors can reach another 1,800 students gathered in the same lecture halls later that same day. Theoretically, a single professor can lecture to a "class" of 3,600 —more students than some teachers confront in decades of teaching.

The heart of the Miami operation lies in the projection core in the center of the octagon. From this core, films, film strips, slides, and television images are projected onto the screens at the front of each lecture hall. Because the projection equipment is behind the screen, students are not distracted or disturbed by mechanical operations.

Through the middle of the octagon

runs a service "spine" housing a television studio, storage areas, facilities for the projection of visual aids, and offices for the 22-man staff of producer-directors, technicians, clerks, and artists who provide back-up services for the teaching staff. (Similar spines run along the sides of rectangular lecture centers on the campuses of the State University of New York.)

For "live" classes, instructors use lecterns on the stages of each auditorium. Each lectern gives the teacher push-button control over lighting and sound levels in the classroom as well as over the projectors and tape recorders behind the screen. In addition, one auditorium has been outfitted with utilities and waste outlets to facilitate science demonstrations.

As might be expected in a pioneering structure, the Miami octagon is not without its critics. Some faculty members are less than enthusiastic about television teaching, while others who favor it complain of conflicts with the technical staff. Still others grumble about the lighting, the size of the seats, and shaky tablet arms (which since have been re-engineered). One local technical journal criticized the building as "heavy-handed" and aesthetically unattractive. Architect Robert Fitch Smith of Miami wishes he could have "done more" with the outside of the building, but explains that the stringencies of the budget did not allow for more.

Nevertheless, University College gets high grades from most of the

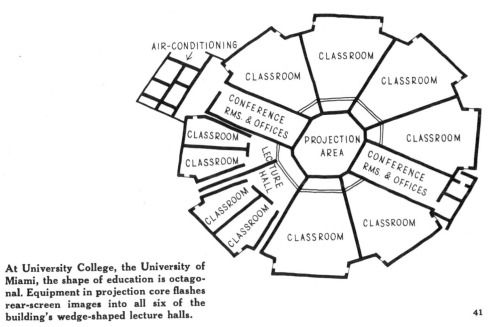

At University College, the University of Miami, the shape of education is octagonal. Equipment in projection core flashes rear-screen images into all six of the building's wedge-shaped lecture halls.

41

Miamians who teach and learn there. "This building has yielded some unexpected educational dividends," said social science professor Robert Munson, one of the faculty's star performers. "With those walls sharply tapering down to the big screen, all eyes naturally focus on the image of the teacher. The effect is like one of those 'Uncle Sam Wants You' posters. You can't get that in the ordinary classroom."

For Professor Munson, one of the major advantages in teaching at University College is that each of his lectures is given a re-run in the afternoon. "I like to watch the tape showing," he confessed. "It lets me look for weak spots in my lecture. I can also watch the reaction of the kids. I don't think the medium bothers them. This is a generation raised on television."

By and large, the students seem to agree. Typically, Barbara Thompson, a junior from Coral Gables, asked, "In a large university with large classes, what difference does it make whether the teacher is there in person or on television? I don't think anyone minds one way or the other."

University College, not surprisingly, has become a pedagogical mecca for educators and technicians concerned with the effectiveness of television as a teaching tool. In its use of television, the new Miami installation is unique. But in its equipment it is just one of many examples of what is called the "systems" approach to audio-visual engineering. Several other institutions have linked up an assortment of electronic devices for use in the classroom and lecture hall. At Teachers College-North, for instance, the Teleprompter Corporation hooked together a $40,-000 system in a 673-seat auditorium. Dubbed "Telemation" by the designers, the system provides for completely integrated and automated rear screen projection of images and sound from an array of motion-picture, slide, and film-strip projectors; stereophonic tape recorders; and closed-circuit television.

The Telemation system makes the instructor the master rather than confused servant of the equipment. Using a remote control or "automated" lectern, the professor can activate appropriate audio-visual devices at moments of his choosing, merely by pressing a button. In more sophisticated applications, the instructor doesn't even have to be present. By placing cue strips on a pre-recorded taping of the lecture, the required audio-visual equipment can be brought into play automatically without the aid of either the professor or a behind-the-scenes technician.

Telemation employs three screens for the simultaneous projection of visual images. The triple images are supposed to reinforce the learning process by enabling a student to quickly compare and contrast different views of the same subject or object. Some audio-visual experts consider the multiple screens as one of the exciting innovations of recent years. However, Professor C. R. Carpenter of Pennsylvania State University, cautions against placing too much emphasis on the sheer number of images and screens.

"It is quite possible," says Professor Carpenter, director of the Division of Academic Research and Services at Penn State, "that the additional screens and display surfaces are more distracting than helpful to the student. There is, I feel, a limit to the amount of information a student should be required to absorb in a limited period of time." The new, $3 million circular lecture center to be built at Penn State will have only two screens in each of its four auditoriums. Moreover, Penn State refuses to commit itself completely to the increasingly popular rear screen projection method. "We'll use the rear screen system," Professor Carpenter said, "but we've made provision for front screen as well. It is a much better means for showing color films frequently used in the art school."

THE ELECTRONIC TUTOR

The electronic tube also has had an impact on individual study, which since the invention of the printing press has been largely limited to books, a student, and a source of light. At Teachers College-North, for example, electronics will be used to lure students to the Q-Spaces. By March, 1964, the college hopes to have eight carrels experimentally outfitted with a set of earphones, a tape recorder, a small television monitor, and a tele-

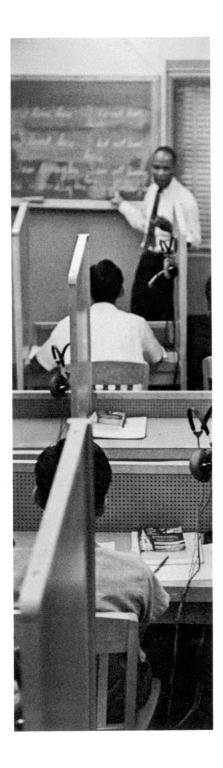

phone-type dial. By dialing a number, students will be able to hook into a master random-access system of tape-recorded instructional materials. They will also be able to tune in one of several closed-circuit television channels featuring a variety of supplementary instructional programs. If the experiment succeeds, both educationally and electronically, all the carrels eventually will be fitted out in the same way.

Florida Atlantic University plans to equip each of the 200 carrels in its learning resources laboratory (a combination classroom and study center) with its own writing surface, tape deck, earphones, television monitor, and either a telephone dial or set of push-buttons. The idea, explained Len Singer, director of Learning Resources, "is that somewhere on campus we will post a daily calendar or menu of what will be available on the 'Quest Channels' at a particular time. Then, a student enrolled in a humanities course can come to the lab, be assigned to a station, press a button or operate a dial, and listen in comfort and privacy to a Shakespearean sonnet on his earphones. Or, if he is in a social science course, he can listen to a Churchill speech or a foreign policy debate. We also anticipate leaving an open channel, so that a student can request the playing of any tape which is catalogued and filed in the library. In this way, if a student wants to come in and hear something like the Mormon Tabernacle Choir, he can do that, too."

Mr. Singer expects that Florida Atlantic will handle its television programing in similar fashion. As many as six closed-circuit channels will be in operation once the video system is established.

Florida Atlantic University will not build a traditional language laboratory as such. The fact that Mr. Singer can refer to such a recent innovation as the language lab as "traditional" may be one measure of the rapidity of change in educational technology. The learning resources laboratory will double as a language lab. "Whenever we need a language lab," Mr. Singer explained, "all we will do will be to bring down an operable wall and section off 50 to 75 of the 200 stations in the learning lab. We don't intend to put expensive electronic facilities into a language classroom and then see them lie idle half the day."

Ultimately, Florida Atlantic's Q-Spaces will be equipped with a system through which students will respond to questions pre-programed into the audio and visual tapes. Such a system has already been developed by Corrigan and Associates of San Mateo, California. In the Corrigan system, when the student presses the correct button to respond to a question, a green light flashes on a plate attached to the television monitor. A wrong answer produces a red light. The student continues to press buttons until he finally gets the green light. However, each time he presses a button, a hole is punched in an IBM card. When the telecast is over, the professor (or studio technician) presses a button, releasing the cards for machine grading.

Less elaborate and less automated response systems are being installed in the new lecture halls at Miami, Texas, Teachers College-North, and Penn State, where Ray Carpenter built the forerunner of all such systems in 1948. In the live teaching situation, the response systems can be used both for grading purposes and to help the instructor determine how well his lecture is being received. Several commercial response systems feed student answers into a box or meter on the instructor's lectern. If a large number of students press the wrong button, in response to a simple verbal or visual question about the lecture, the instructor will see the result on his lectern. Then, theoretically, he can pause, go back over his material, and ask the same question a second time.

"In the old days," said one professor, "students were asked to raise their hands if they were unable to follow what the teacher was saying. That was a little like asking a group of women at a party to raise their hands if they felt they were not as well dressed as the other women there. You never got much of a response. The electronic system should make the problem of determining who has gotten what out of a lecture a little less embarrassing to the student and a little less frustrating to the teacher."

Response systems may help universities to determine the precise educational value of the expensive audio-visual systems they are installing in their classrooms and lecture halls. Just such an evaluation is under way at the University of Wisconsin's School of Education, where a Telemation system has been in use since 1961 in a 277-seat auditorium. During the spring of 1962, Dr. Michael Petrovich presented an automated and pre-recorded course in Russian history. The tape carried not only Dr. Petrovich's voice, but appropriate background music such as Tchaikovsky's "1812 Overture." On the triple screens, students viewed an integrated succession of maps, pictures, charts, diagrams, names, and dates designed to reinforce the verbal presentation. Queried at the end of the semester, 69 of the 73 students indicated that, given a choice, they would prefer a Telemated presentation to a simple lecture.

Not that the system at Wisconsin is perfect; far from it. The visuals are somewhat crude and frequently irrelevant. Many of them, particularly those thrown on the smaller screens are not legible from the rear of the not-too-large auditorium. But Dr. John Guy Fowlkes, the moving spirit behind the program, explained: "We're not wedded to any one screen size, method of projection, lighting, or type of auditorium. This is a multi-media laboratory in human learning. We want to find out what effect visual and audio aids have on learning. We want to know, among other things, what kind of aids should be used, how many should be used during each class session, and how long they should be kept on the screen."

Similarly, Chicago Teachers College-North has not been without problems in making proper use of its Telemated auditorium. During the first year of operation the system rarely was used as it should have been. The reason was simple: no one had time to give it much thought. Instead of exploring the potentials of the automated system and multiple visual images, most of the lectures in the auditorium were presented in rather traditional fashion. "What we should have done," said Dr. Jerry Sachs, dean of the academic program, "was to have found out what we needed and wanted in a large auditorium and then gone ahead and built it. We're pleased with what we have, but we now have to adapt our programs to the auditorium, instead of the other way around."

But progress is being made. Already, one English course has been fully programed to take advantage of the system. Other courses will be adapted in the future as Robert Walker, the industrious young speech teacher who directs the auditorium operations, orients the faculty in its functions. Mr. Walker feels that, once this happens and once the auditorium is equipped with a response system, it will begin to fulfill its purpose: involving the student directly and actively in the learning process. "When the student is brought into the lecture with the response system and when we use the

Telemation at work in University of Wisconsin art lecture.

multiple screens to produce a panorama of sensory experiences rather than to illustrate a verbal point," he said, "then we will have begun to exploit the potential of Telemation."

Obviously the electronic teaching facility requires an expertise generally not found among most college faculties. For a system such as Telemation to function as it should, a technical staff must work in close conjunction with the faculty. Adrian TerLouw, educational consultant at Eastman Kodak, believes that, even in the smallest college, a minimum staff of three would be needed to provide proper back-up service for the faculty.

The technicians, in the ideal arrangement, should do more than run the machines and produce the audiovisuals. They must, in Mr. TerLouw's view, be prepared to work with the faculty in the time-consuming and sometimes painful task of reorganizing a course for audio-visual presentation. All too frequently, there has been only token integration of audio-visuals in lectures. Mr. TerLouw, who has worked directly with several universities in revamping courses for audio-visual presentation, insists that the instructor must sit down with the technical specialist and learn to look at his course material from the student's point of view. This, he says, takes a good deal of the professor's time and a large measure of professional and intellectual adjustment. "The criteria of a good lecture is not what happens to the professor's ego, but what happens to the student's mind," said Mr. Ter-Louw. "The teacher must learn that he is just one part of the learning process. He must, in other words, learn to keep his mouth shut."

THE RELUCTANT PROFESSORS

In many hallowed halls of ivy, this prospect is about as inviting as a fellowship to the South Pole. The truth is that many scholars have a highly un-communal feeling about television and other audio-visual devices. They view the new gadgetry with a combination of discomfort, disdain, and distrust. The ever growing shortage of teachers renders groundless the professional fear of technological unemployment. But it doesn't alter the professional attitude toward the machine. Elwin Stevens of the State University of New York commented: "We can build all kinds of new spaces for learning, but getting the professors to teach in them is another, and thus far unsolved, problem."

Doubtless, the cold war between the scholar and the machine will intensify as the electronic revolution accelerates on the campus. It will be difficult to disabuse some faculty of the notion that an audio-visual system consists of a hare-brained student lugging a half-broken projector into a dimly lit room to show a scratchy old film that is as academically pertinent as a "Three Stooges" short. But the state of educational technology has come a long way from this doleful image, and it will travel considerably further in the years to come. Just beyond the frontier of learning lies an educational tool that has barely been explored by the colleges and universities: the computer.

Data processing machines are making up payrolls, writing checks, and handling other administrative chores in higher education. But few institutions have explored the computer's possibilities as a teaching device. Philip Lewis, director of the Bureau of Instructional Materials for the Chicago Board of Education, says the day is not far off when "closed-circuit television and the computer will be employed along with scientific programing to determine important ways in which instruction can be individualized for each student — the teacher modifying sequences based upon regular checks of progress, and the computer itself modifying presentations automatically as a result of the success or failure of student responses."

There is promise that in the near future the computer will be in use in a good many college classrooms across the country. But there is reason to question whether equipment and programing costs ever will be reduced enough to put the computer within the reach of all colleges or the most advanced computer technology within reach of any of them.

One story making the rounds of faculty dining rooms, concerns the

bright young instructor of 25 years hence who becomes appalled at the cost of equipping each student with an electronic carrel, each classroom with automated audio-visual systems, and each building with computers and color television receivers and transmitters. One evening, adding up all the costs and dividing them by the number of students at the college, a startling idea strikes the young teacher. The next morning he rushes in to see his dean and announces: "Look, instead of spending all this money on operable walls, revolving stages, and coaxial cables, why don't we just divide up the student body into groups of 25 or 30 and put each group into a small room with a live Ph.D.? I don't know how the faculty will like the idea, but it's worth trying."

The story has a simple moral—there still is much to be said for the old-fashioned classroom and the old-fashioned "live" teacher. Any student who has ever sat within a few feet of a really great teacher—a Samuel Eliot Morison at Harvard, a Frederick Pottle at Yale—knows that there is an indefinable magic in the human presence that no electronic tube can ever duplicate. If the human presence made no difference, the legitimate theater would have disappeared during the nickelodeon era. Clearly, many professors are reluctant to introduce technology into their classrooms not because they fear for their jobs or their status or because they do not understand the machine. They fear something else entirely—the dehumanizing of one of the most human of all experiences—learning.

There seems to be a need, therefore, to plan the new, "automated" instructional facility with man — or boy and girl — uppermost in mind. The coldly perfect building doesn't seem to fit into the environment of learning. The University of Miami discovered this in its highly efficient and functional University College. The problem was that, if the televised lectures in the auditorium became too slick and too perfect, student attention tended to wane. The solution was to program small but obvious errors into the scripts to keep the audiences mentally alert. Practice had made Miami instructors too perfect. The deliberate "slips" somehow made them more human and more believable.

The experience of the University of Miami has also proved the wisdom, in an era of large group instruction, of following up mass lectures with frequent face-to-face contacts between student and teacher. The "University College auditorium," explained Dean Paul Vonk, "has enabled us to expose more students to our best teachers and at lower cost than would be possible by traditional methods. But it would be of little educational value if we did not supplement the televised lectures with smaller seminars and laboratories and frequent student-faculty conferences."

What emerges from the present ferment in teaching practices, and consequently in facilities, is not a simple answer to tomorrow's problems. A drive for increased efficiency, both in teaching and learning, the utilization of more educational tools, and at the same time a growing concern for the individual and for amenity, seem to offer a series of basically conflicting factors. One of the great challenges to education, and to architecture, will be to reconcile these factors in a new synthesis over the remaining years of this century. To develop a new balance in education between the human and economic factors, in the face of the pressures created by enrollment growth and faculty shortages, is the key issue.

Ultimately, each college or university must develop its own educational programs and, from them, determine what form its buildings will take and how they will be equipped. The most successful instructional facilities are more than bricks and mortar. When they are appropriate to the individual college, they can become teaching tools in themselves.

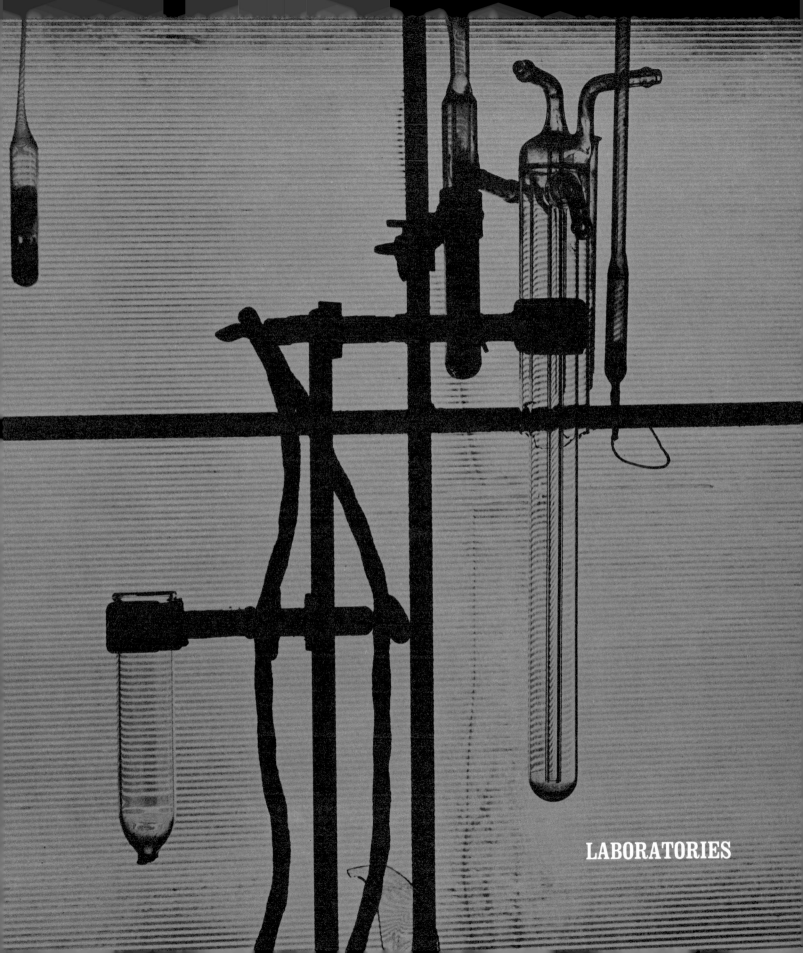

LABORATORIES

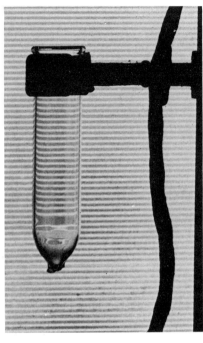

LABORATORIES
by
Bernard Asbell

A college science building, besides being a house of learning, is an assertion that human beings are committed to taking charge of their natural environment. It is an irony of campus architecture, therefore, that teachers and students are often entrapped by the man-made environment of their science buildings.

At the most celebrated place of learning in the Western Hemisphere, Harvard University, the 40-year-old Mallinckrodt chemistry building is a typical example. Externally the strong, staid building is harmonious with its neighboring structures. Its windows perforate the red brick walls with precise evenness, conforming exactly with the history building, the administration buildings, the dormitories. Inside,

however, the scientists pay dearly in disorder for the architect's devotion to exterior neatness. The windows, so pleasing to the passerby on the outside, bring little light to the inside. Rooms and labs are dreary, cluttered, painted in the gloomiest greens and grays. The windows succeed only in destroying the usefulness of interior walls. Shelves run up the walls in crazy, patternless pursuit of those spaces not stolen by windows.

If the outside appearance is strong, the inside ·is virtually indestructible. Laboratory benches are imbedded in the concrete floor, utterly immovable. Fume hoods are encased in vertical columns as solid as support posts. Pipes for water, gases, air, are imbedded in thick walls, like buried treasure,

defying anyone who might dream of getting at them. Each floor is split lengthwise by a center corridor, fixed forever by permanent walls, posts, and plumbing, so that rooms themselves are a petrification of an architect's 40-year-old guess of future needs. As the building was in 1923, so is it now, and so must it be until it crumbles.

Before any reader takes smug comfort in scoffing at Harvard, let it be emphasized that in the twenties *all* science buildings were built that way. Many were built that way in the thirties, forties, and fifties, and some still repeat that basic pattern today.

Harvard, in fact, was one of the first to upset tradition. In the early thirties it pioneered the idea of flexibility in a new biology building. To a visitor walking down its hall, the new building could hardly be distinguished from an old one, for a center corridor still separated two equally wide rows of rooms. The corridor walls still were thick, and concealed a miasma of pipes and wires. But the building was revolutionary because the partitions between rooms were not committed to stand for generation upon generation. They were merely partitions and not encasements for utilities. These partitions were installed, according to a module plan, at distances of 12 feet or multiples of such distances. A single 12-foot module was suitable for an office or dark room. Three module units made a suitable lab for 12 to 20 students. Labs could extend as long as the faculty cared to make them. Walls

51

could be knocked down with comparative ease and rebuilt elsewhere. Utility services were piped to lab benches along the outsides of these partitions, easily tapped, easily removed, and visible to the eye. No one seemed aesthetically upset. Still, the width of any room, whether a small office or lengthy lab, was frozen by the distance between corridor and exterior wall.

This seeming revolution in design was merely a baby step towards real flexibility. Yet today, multimillion dollar, apparently modern, science buildings, with sleek exteriors of glass and stainless steel, are still being built with that same interior pattern.

"Around the world one sees the same costly mistakes repeated while good solutions are not being shared," said architect Philip W. Faulconer recently, before the Royal Institute for Engineering Sciences at Stockholm. Mr. Faulconer had just completed a world-wide inspection of modern science buildings. "It is unfortunate that the technical world, justly proud of its scientific method, often rushes buildings into existence without allowing adequate study and evaluation of previous efforts elsewhere."

A TAKING-OFF POINT: THE FLIGHT DECK

Not long ago a new science building was opened in Boston that smashed the old, frozen patterns. It was built by the Retina Foundation for research in the medical and biological sciences.

True, it is not an instructional building, but it is an advanced model of science building flexibility.

Its architect, H. Peter Klein of Bedford, Mass., a pilot in World War II, determined that the needs of a science building are analogous to those of an aircraft carrier.

"The flight deck of an aircraft carrier," says Mr. Klein, "must be completely open and empty. This corresponds to the unpredictable needs of lab space in a science building. If space is to be fully available for any kind of future use, it must be built open, uninterrupted. Then it can be divided by partitions that may be removed and put up again elsewhere.

"But to make the open flight deck of a carrier useful, the ship needs utilities, power, defense equipment, quarters for its men, and so forth. These are all housed in an isolated superstructure pushed somewhat beyond the edge so it extends over the side of the vessel. A good science building should make a unit of its 'superstructure'—its vertical shafts for services and exhausts, its stairs, rest rooms, and so forth—and get that unit as much out of the way as possible."

Mr. Klein designed a four-story structure, 94 feet square. To reserve every possible inch of his lab building for "flight deck," or research, space, he built a separate, smaller building for a library, lecture rooms, and administrative offices.

Wires and pipes for electricity, liquids, and gases rise from the base-

ment to laboratory floors through two vertical shafts near one side of the building. Rest rooms and a staircase are clustered near them, so the preponderance of floor space is like a great loft.

The space is not used, however, as a loft. It is divided by walls, as removable and interchangeable as parts of an Erector set, into rooms as small as 5 feet square (for photomicrography) and as large as 30 feet square (for a general biochemistry lab). If desired, a general lab could be much larger, with no interruption by walls or vertical utility feeds.

The design of floor space is governed by a strict module of 5'2" north-south and east-west (allowing 2" for partitions). Everything—structural gridwork, floor slabs, movable partitions, width of windows, even dimensions of furniture—relates to the module size. Thus rooms may be rearranged at will to any dimension that is a multiple of 5'2" square.

To bring liquids, gases, and power to any point on a laboratory floor, pipes reach out from the utility cores and run between the beams that suspend the ceilings. Then they reach down and across, fastened to the removable walls, exposed to the eye and easily reached by the hand. Or they may reach *up* to the floor above through any of 115 knockout panels in each floor.

The building is entirely air-conditioned. To prevent fume hoods, which are all movable, from inhaling room

Movable walls lend flexibility to instructional space in Olin Hall, Colorado College.

air and ejecting it from the building, fume hoods "breathe" air through louvers in the exterior walls. Exhaust air from hoods flows through ducts between ceiling beams to any of four concrete towers that rise along the outside walls. These towers can be taken apart, moved, or extended upwards to permit future expansion.

Just as the utilities rise near one side of the building, leaving a large floor area free, the building itself stands on one side of its land site. Its mirror image may be built to the south, doubling the size of each floor. In addition, the existing capacities of structure and utilities permit building two additional floors overhead. These additions would triple the present laboratory space in harmonious extension of the original structure.

The building is unstinted in its components. Its movable walls are sound-insulated with skins of baked-enamel steel. Its windows are double glass panels that enclose venetian blinds, keeping the blinds dust-free. The windows may be swung open for easy cleaning as well as for natural ventilation in case of an air-conditioning breakdown. Suspended acoustic ceiling panels faced with white-enameled steel are easily removed for access to the utility system between the beams. Even the lighting system—fluorescent in the lab areas, incandescent elsewhere—is custom designed for the module pattern.

It would be hard to find a more desirable execution of a science building

for unpredictable uses. Only one fact would prevent almost any college from emulating its design: the building was costly. Laboratory space, including fixed and movable equipment, cost $37.25 per square foot. In contrast, the average cost of a college science building in the northeastern United States in 1960 was $24.80 per square foot. So, builders of college science buildings, who may profitably window shop for ideas at imaginative structures like the Retina Foundation, must also inspect them to help decide what to do without.

FLEXIBILITY FOR WHAT?

Three years ago Colorado College, educating 1,150 students near the slopes of Pike's Peak, received a $1,500,000 gift to erect a sorely needed science building. A faculty committee immediately set about seeking a principle to govern the design of the new structure.

The guiding principle they fixed upon, one which was already becoming the architectural catchword of our time, was flexibility. Science, the committee reasoned, is a rapidly changing collection of knowledge; the techniques of teaching science are themselves undergoing great, unpredictable changes. Whole revolutions may mature in a decade. Yet their new science building, besides serving the needs of today, must suit students and teachers who for the next two decades may not even be born. Clearly the building

must be flexible — conducive to new uses—if its future inhabitants are not to be chained and robbed by obsolete architecture.

The committee invited a half-dozen respected, imaginative architects to be interviewed for the attractive assignment. Each of them readily grasped the notion of flexibility and sparked ideas for accomplishing the difficult goal; that is, each except one. William W. Caudill, a bushy-haired, bramble-browed Texan, gazed at the teachers in faint wonderment as though he were not quite sure what they were talking about. At each mention of the word "flexibility," he asked, "What do you mean by that?"

Impatiently the teachers enumerated a long list of attributes of a flexible building. Mr. Caudill dutifully jotted them down, then read the list back. The list, he showed them, contained contradictions, solutions to problems they did not face, and solutions that concealed other problems. Furthermore, each item in the list was accompanied by a cost, and the ideas far outran the $1,500,000 budget.

"It's obvious," he said, "that flexibility is a big word that means many more things than you, perhaps any college, can buy. In fact, it means more things than you need. I suggest we start all over again and ask, 'Flexibility for what?'"

Mr. Caudill (who wound up getting the job) and the faculty committee soon set to work designing an unusual, low-cost building—$19.66 per square foot, including equipment. It was opened in September 1962. The building, which will be described later, was planned, however, only after the faculty committee was required by its architect to dissect the word flexibility into all the major things it may mean.

It may mean expandability. A science building can be designed to accommodate growing enrollments, to double, triple, quadruple in size by extending the building horizontally or upward. Big expansion is an urgent problem to some colleges and universities, but is not sought by certain others, among them, Colorado College.

Flexibility may mean allowing for changes in the relative demand for physics, chemistry, and biology space, or for merging these spaces for biochemistry, biophysics, or physical chemistry. Labs for each of these departments can be designed so they can be taken from one science discipline, and easily re-equipped, assigned to another, or shared.

Flexibility may mean providing each discipline with services it does not now need but may need later: various electrical currents, gases, air withdrawal for fume hoods, air conditioning. Since these may one day be needed in any lab, are they to be installed now for ready use, or merely roughed in to be tapped if and when needed? Are they to be roughed in so that services can be provided easily on a few days' notice, or a few hours, or even minutes? Is the tapping of a service to be accomplished by the building

engineer, or shall it be made so easy that even an instructor or responsible student, engaged in a special, individual research project, can do it by himself without delay?

Flexibility may mean building labs without labels, available to all departments. When a physics period ends, the lab may be converted to chemistry or biology in a few minutes. Thus, valuable lab space need not stand idle.

Flexibility may mean building large instructional labs that easily divide into clusters of small research labs, and vice versa. In interchanging large rooms and small ones, corridors may be shifted this way and that for maximum utility of the floor plan.

All of these flexibilities are practical. But each bears a price tag. Each is important to someone, somewhere. Hardly any college, however, can seriously expect to need them all. So before a college may intelligently decide how much flexibility its science building needs, it must make certain important decisions about itself, its academic character, its future growth, and the place of science instruction in its future.

Chicago architect Walter A. Netsch, Jr., of Skidmore, Owings and Merrill, suggests some basic questions that a faculty committee must ask itself before intelligent planning of a science building can begin:

Does the college plan to grow? If so, how much? A traditionally small college, say of 1,500 students, that is determined to maintain its present size,

can seek entirely different building solutions from a fast-growing campus.

Does the college, whether growing or not, plan to revise the emphasis on science in its curriculum? Will it permit its proportion of science majors to grow?

Does the college now offer postgraduate science study? If so, does it plan expansion of such study? If not, does it plan to introduce it? Obviously, changes in the world of science will be more directly reflected in the equipment needs of advanced students than of undergraduates.

How much research is the science faculty expected to do? Attractive, perhaps expensive, research space may be a critical factor in the department's ability to attract teachers of first quality. (A small college recently succeeded in hiring an eminent biologist engaged in research on monkeys. To get him, the college had to promise space for the monkeys and build a great number of cages.) What limit does the college plan to put on the sophistication of its research environment? Is it prepared to install a radioactive lab, a 7090 computer, a high-speed wind tunnel? Each requires costly provision in the original plan.

How eager is the college to use its lab space efficiently? Efficiency in the use of space, desirable as it appears, may collide with an equally desirable atmosphere of thinking time and research time for the faculty. Many colleges, for example, conduct their science classroom lectures in the morning and lab sessions in the afternoon. Labs stand idle for half of each day. These schools could schedule lab sessions both morning and afternoon, do the same with lectures, and double their efficiency in use of space. This step, however, requires a professor to give two lectures while he now gives one, and two lab sessions instead of one. It would sharply reduce his research time, his leisure, and perhaps his attraction to the job.

What is the attitude of the faculty about the present trend towards independent study? A science department encouraging independent study must be prepared to assign lab benches permanently to individual students using elaborate apparatus. It may wish to wall off many such benches from general labs.

THE SKELETON WITH A BACKBONE

Architect George F. Pierce, Jr., of Pierce and Pierce, Houston, Texas, sifted through problems like these when he was commissioned to produce new space for biology at Rice University, which has 2,000 students. His experience is an informative case study in logical, imaginative planning and an impressive result at a cost of $22 per square foot, including equipment.

Biology courses at Rice have grown from one in 1913 to 16 at present. Today's freshman course has 240 students. Thirty undergraduates major in

biology and almost 100 others are pre-med students. More than a dozen postgraduates, including two or three postdoctoral men, are engaged in research on fellowships and grants from the National Science Foundation, the Atomic Energy Commission, the American Cancer Society, and others.

For years the growing biology department was a tenant of the physics building, each department increasingly squeezed by the other. The biology department wanted to expand its undergraduate courses and further stimulate postgraduate research. Geology had a similar need, and Mr. Pierce was authorized to plan twin buildings for them.

Mr. Pierce embarked on a national tour to inspect the most modern science buildings he could find. "The main thing I learned," he has since observed, "was a lot of things *not* to do." He was appalled at seeing new buildings with spaces frozen by center corridors, permanent walls, interruptions by "superstructure."

In close study with the faculty, Mr. Pierce took up as his first problem the number of floors the new building should have. A one-story structure, they decided, would require excessively long horizontal utility runs, occupy much land, and suffer high heat flow through a large roof. Two stories cut these problems in half and permitted a division of activities: large, beginning classes on the first floor, research on the second. A two-story building, however, would require 300 square

feet for stairs and the large cost of an elevator, an uneconomic penalty for one additional floor.

Extending the elevator and stairs for a third floor would be a minor cost, easily outbalanced by further savings in horizontal utility runs, roof area, and exterior materials. Rooms requiring ground floor space because of large traffic or heavy items of delivery comprised one-third of the entire space need, so there was no point in considering a fourth floor. The building would have three floors.

Then Mr. Pierce brought off an architectural coup that at once cut the cost of operating the building and at the same time vastly enhanced its usefulness. Sunlight on the south length had to be shaded to prevent an excessive heat flow into rooms. A good shading device for southern exposures was a brow, a horizontal overhang between each pair of floors. At the same time Mr. Pierce was puzzling over the fundamental problem of uninterrupted floor space. This suggested getting rid, if possible, of the traditional center corridor. Ideally, a corridor would run along one side of the building. The south side was preferable for a corridor, reserving the north wall for its superior room lighting. The solution was evident. The overhangs on the south could also serve as the floors of exterior corridors, actually outside the building. Vertical cement louvers would shield the corridors from blowing rain and be attractive to the eye.

So far, the interior space was entirely undisturbed. But how about the need for stairs, elevators, rest rooms? Mr. Pierce reasoned that if the corridors were outside of work spaces, the logical place for stairs, elevators, and rest rooms was outside also. He placed them beyond the edge of the outside corridor in a vertical column—a striking imitation of the superstructure of an aircraft carrier.

The remaining major problem of structure was how to make utilities efficiently available to every square foot of lab space. At Rice, most utilities originate at a central power plant and are distributed around the campus through underground tunnels. This tunnel could run beneath the biology building for its entire length. A series of vertical chases could bring utilities up to lab floors.

Mr. Pierce designed a vertical chase about 6 feet square to contain all wires, pipes, and ducts needed for the 50-foot width of the building and for 28 feet of its length. Duplicates of this chase would be located at 28-foot intervals. These would run down the center of the building, like distant vertebrae in its spine, yet hardly restrict the possible room layouts. The chases would also serve as center supports from basement to roof.

Each pipe and conduit in the chase would be painted in a code color for easy identification and would occupy an identical position in each chase. Its outlet would be at a code height, i.e., acid waste, 4 inches above the floor; hot water, 8 inches, etc., identical in

Vertical chases, right and rear center, carry utilities up through Rice University biology building.

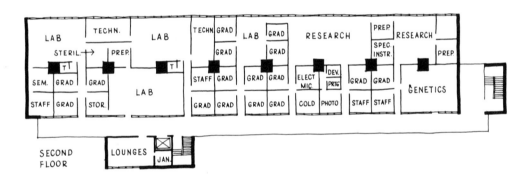

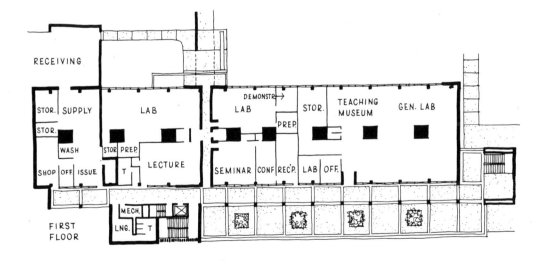

each chase. But the chases would not include all utilities for which a need is foreseen. Instead, *space is to be reserved* in each. Only those presently needed are to be installed and others will be, if and when needed.

Tapping into the chase for a utility service is an easy matter. The surface of a chase is composed of panels mounted by the turn of a large screw. A half-dollar is an adequate screw driver.

Room partitions are made of inexpensive, durable composition board. They are joined by Unistrut braces which also hold fittings to support horizontal pipes for running exposed utilities from the chase to any point in the laboratory area.

Each chase contains its own blower for discharging poisonous gases into the air at the roof. The blower operates only if a fume hood connected to that chase is in use. Even greater economy is applied to air conditioning. Each chase is equipped for·four cool air blowers, each cooling a floor area of 14′ x 25′. Thus a small cluster of offices or a medium size lab may be cooled by flicking the switch of one blower, wasting no cool air in neighboring rooms when it is not needed.

With this plan, floors of 50-foot width and almost 250-foot length are open to almost limitless potential of room arrangements, punctuated only by the 28-foot intervals of the chases. Almost never does a lab require more space than 28 by 50 feet. In the rare instance when one does, one sizeable

post is hardly an inconvenience, particularly when it is dispensing readily available services to nearby work stations. The floor diagram, preceding page, illustrates the variety of possible room arrangements. Land is available west of the building for expansion. To expand, all that is needed is an extension of length and a continuation of the spinal column of utilities.

THE SKELETON
LIKE A GRASSHOPPER'S

At Colorado College, architect Caudill and the faculty considered a spinal arrangement like Rice's. But despite the comparative floor freedom afforded by chases spaced at 28 feet, they decided to avoid even the possibility of a handicap to complete maneuverability.

The decision entailed sacrifices, but they got what they wanted. First, at an extra cost of a few cents per square foot they selected pre-stressed concrete ceiling beams, eliminating the need for center support posts. But they still faced the major problem of where to install their utility chases.

They decided, surprisingly, to hide the utilities in the walls. This may sound like a throwback to the twenties, but is quite the opposite. Instead of freezing the pipes in permanent interior partitions, they surrounded their open floor with utilities in the *exterior* walls—not one exterior wall, but *two*. The real exterior wall is of brick facing.

Two feet inside it, leaving space for a man to walk and work, an inner wall is built of removable panels of inexpensive asbestos-cement board. Within these walls a vertical cluster of pipes and wires rises every 10 feet, easily tapped and extended horizontally into any of the four floors of lab space.

A biology instructor, studying the plan, aptly remarked, "Why, it's like the exoskeleton of a grasshopper. The bones are all in the outer skin." The design has been called exoskeleton ever since.

The double wall is more than a mere cache for pipes and wires. It is also a repository for special equipment which might otherwise clutter up a lab. At each floor level a kind of catwalk is installed in the wall, strong enough to support generators, vacuum pumps, bottled gas, and motors required for individual research projects. The chemistry department decided to install an ordinary dishwasher for lab glassware. They merely removed a wall panel and shoved the machine into the wall, its door conveniently facing into the lab.

The main sacrifice, if it is a sacrifice, entailed by the exoskeleton plan is its sparseness of windows. The building is almost entirely dependent on artificial light. But use of lively color—yellows, browns, blues, and whites—helps establish distinct atmospheric areas for different activities. It is a warm, cheerful place. At seemingly random points on each floor, openings were allowed in the outer shell for win-

Technician installs utility line in double-walled "exoskeleton" of Colorado College science building. Windows, like the one at left, are recessed the depth of the double wall, and add dramatic architectural effect.

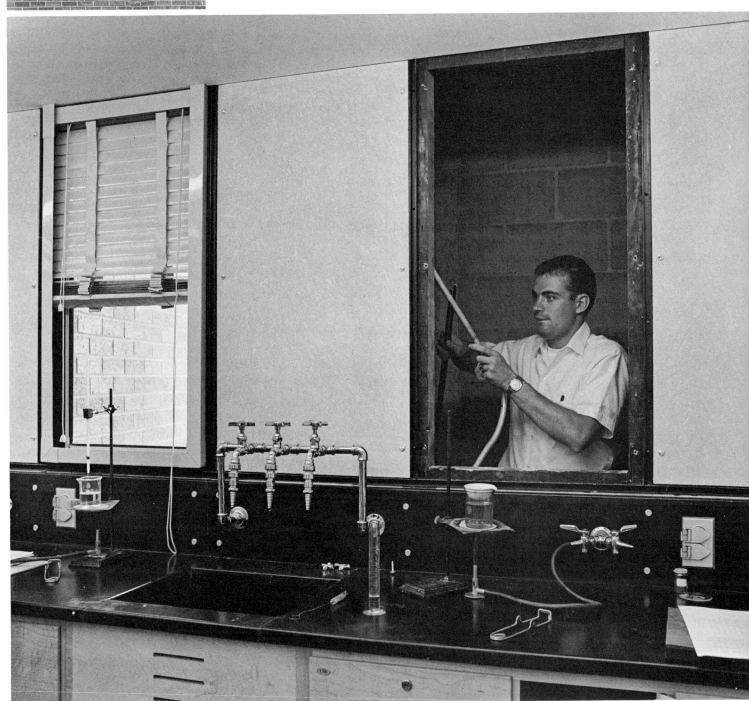

dows installed in the inner walls. Bordering these windows, brick fills the spaces between the walls, giving the illusion of great thickness and strength. Quite accidentally, but rather pleasing to its occupants, the facade suggests the appearance of a great *adobe,* linking it with the heritage of the area. The biologists, occupying the top floor, were less keen than the physicists or chemists about the near-windowless plan. So the fourth floor has almost as many windows as the other floors combined. This irregularity adds, oddly, to the building's architectural interest. A counterpoint to the solid brick theme is also provided by a translucent, corrugated, glass box bulging from the fourth floor, the biology department's built-in greenhouse.

To encourage maximum utilization of space, the planners isolated on the first floor several functions that are used in common by all science departments. These include all general classrooms and a large, unlabeled lab with about a dozen stations. These stations will be assigned to researchers working on projects that overlap the traditional disciplines of physics, chemistry, and biology. Their work, hopefully, will symbolize the growing synthesis of the sciences. The first floor also contains the sources of utility services, storage, and shops.

Physics occupies the second floor, chemistry the third, and biology, the fourth. Each has a different floor plan according to the department's needs and tastes, and any of the floors may be rearranged—partitions are all movable—at will.

Whereas many old buildings have too many permanent walls, Colorado College has even reduced the placement of movable partitions. "A science building," says physics professor Wilbur H. Wright, chairman of the faculty building committee, "must not only avoid being frozen by architecture, but even semantics can get in the way. We often say *room* when we mean *space,* and because we say *room* we isolate a function by walls that we don't need. We asked ourselves 'Why does a balance room have to be a *room?'* Now we have a balance *space* in a general lab. It's much easier for everyone to get to and use. Also we have to be prepared for the uses of certain rooms to disappear without getting stuck with useless rooms. We used to need 'cold rooms' for cryogenics. In the last couple of years we've been able to buy low temperature liquefied gases, protected in vacuum-lined containers. We use them in normal space. We don't need a cryogenics room anymore. The Polaroid camera and electronic recorders of isotopes are making a lot of darkrooms useless. Changes like that will keep happening at a rapid rate, so removable walls will become more important all the time."

The growth of independent study is often used as a reason to encourage movable partitions, so an individual researcher can easily be isolated by walls. But Colorado College makes a

Biology facilities, including greenhouse (facing page), occupy third floor of Olin Hall.

virtue of removing walls between researchers. The physics department set up a long, U-shaped lab at the end of its floor. Faculty researchers work at one end, side by side in the open. Next are senior student researchers, working with nearly identical equipment, helping them identify their work with that of the professionals. Beyond them are the advanced juniors. Presumably, seldom would more than four or five researchers be working in any given hour. In theory, each would be influenced by his awareness of the others. Time will tell if the system is advantageous.

On the same theme, the physics faculty avoids labeling the functions of labs, such as optics or electronics. Instead they have a senior and a junior lab for independent study, one where the individual is relatively free, the other where he requires supervision. Because the specialties are intermixed, each student's awareness and interest in the specialty of his neighbor is heightened. Thus interdisciplinary generalization is encouraged.

"We went as far as the faculty would let us go," says architect Caudill, "in integrating the disciplines. But there are no built-in architectural blocks against their going further."

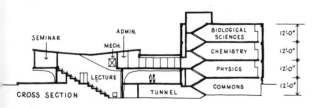

Cross section of Colorado College science building.

THE SKELETON WITH A RIB CAGE

Features of both the Rice and Colorado structures are combined to form a third kind of basic format at the new eight-floor chemistry building of the University of California at Berkeley. There, the San Francisco architectural firm of Anshen and Allen left floor spaces uninterrupted by using what might be called a "rib cage" plan. They, too, brought up their utilities along the outside walls. But instead of putting the bones into the skin—and eliminating the profuse use of windows—they encased the bones in a series of vertical pylons along each side of the structure, with glass between the pylons. The exterior columns are not unlike the interior ones at Rice, except that the exterior arrangement requires two rows of pylons instead of Rice's single spine.

To summarize: the Retina Foundation, with comparatively small, square floors, contains two utility columns inside the building, but away from its center; columns for exhaust ducts are on the outside. The Rice building has a spine of utility columns at 28-foot intervals, feeding outward to surrounding floor space. The exoskeleton Colorado building encases its utilities in a double exterior wall and feeds inward. The Berkeley building also feeds inward, but from a rib cage of two outside rows of columns. All are committed to maximum flexibility of room sizes, relying chiefly on nonpermanent partitions and exposed, wall-mounted utility feed lines.

TOOLS FOR FREEING SPACES

Freeing of floor space for changing needs is not the only path to flexibility. Inventiveness in the choice of equipment can work wonders, sometimes at no extra cost, in enhancing the usefulness of expensive building space. Colorado College equipped its lab benches with drafting stools that swivel in the style of office chairs. An instructor may call for attention and students readily swivel around to face him, comfortably and with no commotion. This simple device encourages on-the-spot lecturing in the lab on procedural problems that might otherwise have to be postponed for classroom time; thus the lab doubles as impromptu lecture space.

The lab-and-lecture functions are even more tightly combined at the Air Force Academy at Colorado Springs. The Academy's method may be considered by some an inefficient use of space, but the faculty has found it effective educationally. Labs have 12 student stations, thus classes are smaller than in most schools. Each lab adjoins a small classroom with 12 tablet-arm chairs. Students are not scheduled for one period of lecture and another of lab. They simply have a period of physics, or chemistry, or biology, each of which may be for lecture or lab or a combination of both. Movement from one room to another is accomplished in seconds. The room arrangement encourages a marriage of theory and practice. Frequently, a student finishes a lab experiment and steps into the classroom to sit down and write up his notes. Similar arrangements are found at Swarthmore and El Camino Colleges and at Indiana University.

The Air Force system illustrates how a tradition is often followed blindly until a hardship forces re-examination of it. Before the Air Force Academy campus was opened, the faculty and cadets were cramped in unsuitable quarters at Lowry Field, Denver. They were forced—by the closeness of permanent walls—to keep classes small, and were forced by a shortage of rooms to combine lab and lecture spaces. They found the lab-lecture combination with small groups so advantageous educationally that they instructed their architects, Skidmore, Owings and Merrill, to embody the method permanently in their new building. The experience makes one wonder how many traditions have never been questioned merely because obvious hardship was not present to force the discovery of new, perhaps better, ways.

Many teachers would argue that lab and classroom functions cannot be combined because chemical odors would be disturbing during lectures. This problem is not present at the Air Force Academy, and surprisingly, the labs don't even have fume hoods. The faculty had the ingenuity to determine that gases used in undergraduate work are heavier than air, therefore tend to settle at the surface of the lab bench. They designed a bench with small, built-in exhaust vents which constantly sweep gases from the table top. The labs are refreshingly free of chemical odor.

Efficient utilization of labs is a particularly pressing problem to a small institution such as Drew University at Madison, New Jersey. With less than 1,000 students and in need of a new science building, President Robert F. Oxnam was pained by the prospect of separate costs for physics, chemistry, and biology labs, each of which would be in use only a small amount of the time. He commissioned the A. B. Stanley Co., lab equipment makers of Chestnut Hill, Massachusetts, to design a multiple-use lab bench, convertible from physics to chemistry in the few minutes between class periods, and similarly from chemistry to biology. Work on the design is now under way. Modular, changeable room dimensions are the theme of the building plans being drawn by the architects, La Pierre and Litchfield of New York, so the building will be ready for unforeseen uses.

Multiple use of benches could intensify a problem, a rather silly one when it is examined, that has long reduced the utilization of old-style labs. The traditional lab bench is outfitted with drawers for equipment, usually one for each student. The number of students who may use a bench during a semester is limited by the number of drawers it contains. Many a faculty has argued the need of an entirely new lab, not because the time in its old lab was all scheduled, but because the drawers were all gone.

For Drew University, the Stanley Co. is designing its multi-use bench with no drawers at all. Drawers will be stored in a wall cupboard, to be removed by a student and taken to his bench. If space ever runs out, a cupboard will be added. Even one-man labs for independent study may enjoy multiple use, accommodating different students in different periods, when a student may clear his bench and slide his equipment into a cupboard.

The Air Force Academy attacked the problem of bench drawers in another, but equally simple way. All students use the same test tubes, beakers, ring stands, and clamps—the usual paraphernalia used by students in introductory courses. In the last five minutes of a period the student is required to clean his equipment and lay it out in a single drawer for the next man. True, occasionally a piece is broken. But replacement of the piece, even at the school's expense rather than the student's, is far cheaper than building and maintaining vast storage space for duplicates of low-cost items. Also, the total inventory of small equipment is reduced to a fraction of the usual quantity.

In a different, highly inventive way, the University of Illinois undergraduate division at Chicago found it can multiply the use of labs by clever use of its storage space. Two faculty members, O. L. Railsback and H. M. Skadeland, have adapted the "lazy susan" principle to setting up lab equipment. The closest parallel is an Automat restaurant. In an Automat, a cylinder containing shelves displays sandwiches to a customer on one side, while shelves on the opposite side face the kitchen for refilling. On the same principle, a three-section rotating device is installed in a partition between a bench and storage room. Each section is fitted with adjustable shelves about three feet wide. While a student works with equipment mounted on the shelves that face him, two other sets of shelves are turned toward the storage room where an attendant may simultaneously be setting up equipment for future periods. Between the periods he turns the device, called a Roto Lab, at each bench, either manually or electrically, and lo, an entirely new lab is ready for a new class. The Roto Lab units are being built by Hamilton Manufacturing Co.

There are other developments that bear watching, although few educators as yet expect them to become standard practice in science instruction. These developments may, however, be useful where expansion in enrollment outruns the availability of lab space.

One is elimination of lab work altogether, substituting demonstration by an instructor. This has been done in some colleges for elementary courses for students not majoring in science. The Air Force Academy, however, tested the demonstration approach on its most promising science students. Of 750 freshmen last year, 125 passed an American Chemical Society exam qualifying them for an accelerated course. Except for qualitative analysis,

the students did no lab work. The freshman course was completed in half its usual time. The mean score of the 125 students in the ACS standardized final exam placed the group in the 93rd percentile for the nation. The faculty has concluded that the students suffered no apparent loss from the lack of lab work. In another instance, 25 upperclassmen earned the right to take physical chemistry as an extra elective. Because of their tight schedules, they had no time for lab work. Again, their final results indicated no apparent loss of comprehension. However, many scientists feel that eliminating lab work emasculates science instruction.

To improve and standardize the quality of lecture-demonstrations, the Commission on College Physics Teaching is investigating the use of short instructional films. Such films may last only a minute or so, demonstrating one step in an experiment. The films may be rolled in an automatic, individual viewing device. A student having difficulty may look in the proper viewer and, at the press of a button, see a film demonstrating a procedure that concerns him. The Air Force Academy has used this method, to aid lab work rather than substituting for it, and reports success.

Another development that may deemphasize the scheduled lab period is the advent of the lab kit. A group of educators financed by the National Science Foundation has developed experimental kits in electronics and optics. The electronics kit, contained in

an easily portable pegboard-type box, contains transistors, resistors, diodes, etc.—the makings of any common circuit. These circuits are demonstrated by a lecturer in class. Then the student takes the kit home or to his dormitory room, pegs components into the perforations of the box, jacks them together, and brings the completed circuits back to the instructor for inspection. Cost of the kit is about $25. At the end of a semester, usable parts of both kits may be repurchased by the department and, with replacement parts added, be sold to another student.

AND SPEAKING OF BEAUTY

The foregoing extended discussion of the problems of planning science buildings has emphasized mechanical requirements. Little has been said on the subject of beauty.

Beauty in a science building, as in any building, was sharply defined by Louis H. Sullivan in only four words: "Form always follows function." But William Caudill, who would not accept undefined use of the word flexibility, is also hesitant about accepting Sullivan's enunciation without a hard look. The important requirement of a new science building, he reasons, is that its function must permit change and, as a result, its function is at least partially unknown. Therefore, says Mr. Caudill, Sullivan's dictum should be revised: "Form *allows* function." The beauty, integrity, and permanence that a science building deserves should not be a reflection of frozen function, but should derive from the excitement of change that its flexible interior must allow.

"Stage-setting and self-deception," adds architect Philip W. Faulconer, "produced effective palaces, but have no place in design for technology. Pipes, ventilators, tanks are essential elements. All that is necessary is a sense of order and logic. For example, corridors need not be as high as adjoining laboratories, so the overhead space can be used for ducts, pipes, and cables, easily accessible for modifications. Paint them dark and direct all

Olin Hall of Science — Colorado College.

light downward where it is needed, and the utilities disappear. External utilities such as chimneys, cooling towers and water reservoirs can become objects of beauty, such as the graceful brick towers at Chester and Calder in England (or the graceful concrete ones at the Retina Foundation and the University of California chemistry building) or reservoirs which are located as reflecting basins in landscaping schemes."

Yet architects often talk about mechanical requirements as though they were unpleasant necessaries that confuse the higher problem of good design. "The trouble with architects," science educators often say, "is that they don't know anything about science." This is undoubtedly as true as its converse: scientists don't know anything about architecture.

The wall that separates men who need a science building from those who plan it must be made as collapsible and removable as those in the new, improved science building that both hope to erect.

Addressing himself to scientists on faculty building committees, Mr. Caudill says: "Don't tell your architect to go and work in isolation. We want to build a building for the people who are going to use it. We have to solve *your* problems. We can only do this by studying your art, and by your studying ours. Each of us has to read about the other and visit buildings—not just one or two, but many; old ones as well as new—to find out how buildings got in the way of their users, and how others didn't.

"Don't tell your architect you want a building like the one at Carleton or Colorado College. If theirs is a good one, it came out of a clear communication of their needs. We want to help you develop a clear communication of yours. On the other hand, the architect has to distinguish between what you say you want and what you may really need. The more you teach us, the better we can do it."

In planning the Colorado College exoskeleton building, Mr. Caudill culminated weeks of research by scheduling what he calls a "squatter's week." It is an intensive time of birth of an architectural plan, complete with labor pains.

A design team from his firm, Caudill, Rowlett and Scott of Houston, set up an office in a temporary building on the exact location of the projected science building at Colorado Springs. On Monday a team of 29 architects and teachers reviewed their research, defined broad objectives, listed space needs, compared space needs with budget, re-examined space needs and reduced them to fit the budget, probed into the meaning of flexibility, and discussed how to locate and route major utilities. All in a day; needless to say, the day ended early the next morning.

On Tuesday, architect team members met in small groups with faculty team members to zero in on specific departmental needs in light of reduced space specifications. Then the critical stage of sketching began. The utility plan and space allotments were translated into section and floor plans.

On Wednesday, the faculty team looked over the sketches, evaluated, reconsidered, criticized, suggested. Communication was now in full flow. Two diverse disciplines, commonly engaged, were reacting to each other, learning from each other, developing common language. In the afternoon, the architects revised their sketches. (The afternoon lasted until early morning.)

On Thursday, the revised plans were criticized again, touched up, and concluded. A final preliminary plan, including perspective sketches and section drawings, was prepared for presentation to the trustees and administration. Mr. Caudill retired at one in the morning, much earlier than his co-workers.

On Friday morning, the formal presentation was made.

"It was almost like a psychoanalysis," says Dr. Wilbur Wright, chairman of the faculty committee. "That's how intense it was. But what came out of it was *our* building. Every time we raised a problem it was thrown back at us to help solve according to our needs. We discovered and discussed problems we had never dreamed of, the function of a wall, the assumption that we need a room when what we really need is a space, flexibility we can use and flexibility we don't need. We were forced to examine everything, and so were they. I never had a greater educational experience in my life. If America is ever to have a truly indigenous architecture it will grow out of such close, intensive exchange between users and designers. We really feel this building belongs on our campus because it came out of us."

Neither Dr. Wright nor Mr. Caudill—nor, for that matter, members of the joint team—is sure that their exoskeleton and its accompanying paucity of external glass will at first delight the eyes of all campus strollers. But they are confident in its rightness of design. As form follows function, they believe, affection will follow their building's form.

The building is surely a rare example of the kind advocated by a speaker at the seventh annual workshop of the Council for the Advancement of Small Colleges held in the summer of 1962 at the Massachusetts Institute of Technology. Don L. Davis, associate director of the School Planning Laboratory at Stanford University, summed up the case for knocking down the walls between architects and teachers when he said:

"It isn't the architect, but the educator and educational specifications (or lack thereof) that give us the buildings with which we are afflicted. When we can tell the architect precisely and effectively what is to take place within a building and for what reason, then I have no doubt that we will get the kinds of facilities that we mostly talk about now."

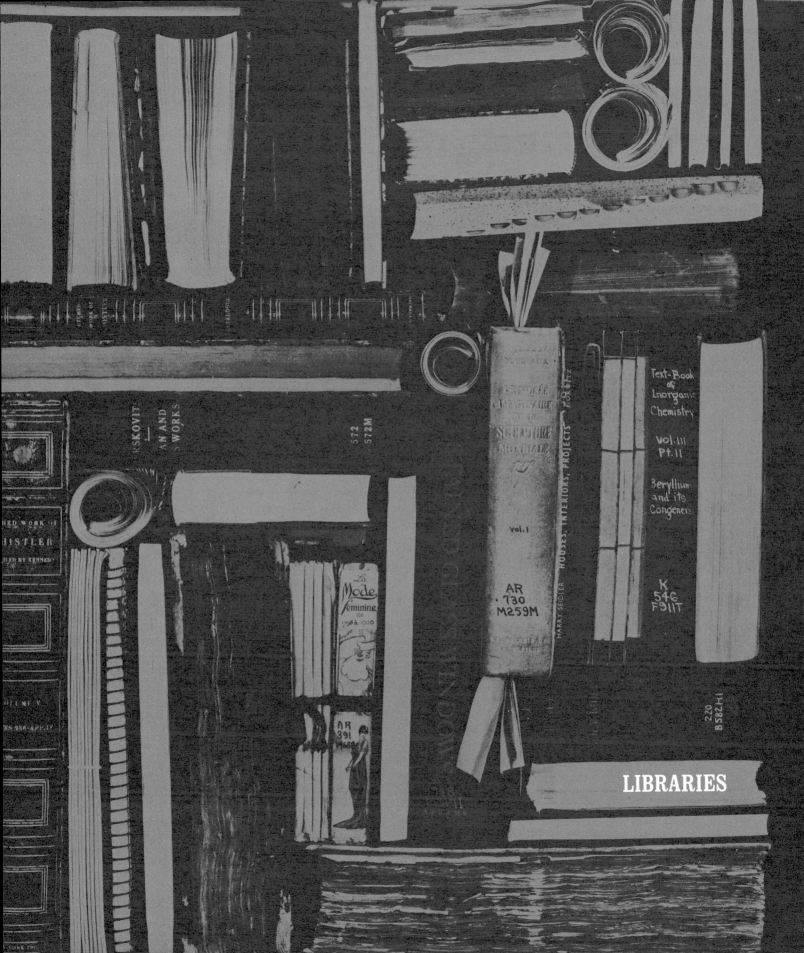

LIBRARIES

LIBRARIES
by
Alvin Toffler

Fifteen years ago a revolution swept the planning of college and university libraries. A new type of library sprang up on the grounds of many campuses —a clean-lined contemporary library that emphasized efficiency and economy, occasionally at the cost of beauty or comfort. Today the initial force of that revolution has spent itself. Campus planners, architects, and librarians are modifying its principles, softening the lines of the revolutionary model, adding grace to its form, and shaping the library to accommodate man in all his individual variety. The result is a more human library than any we have ever known. But already a new revolution is brewing, one that promises to be more profound and far-reaching than any to date. For while the changes of

the recent past adapted the library to man, the coming revolution must adapt the library to the machine. And there are those who insist that this is impossible, that, in fact, the library will be completely swallowed up by the machine.

Some argue forcefully that the library and the book itself are mere relics of an inefficient past, that the job of storing, retrieving, and transmitting information will, in the future, be accomplished without either. They point out that there is nothing inviolable about the book or its storehouse, that cuneiform tablets gave way to papyrus rolls, that medieval manuscripts gave way to books, and that books are already sharing the job of communicating information with other

carriers. Already most libraries store records, tapes, films, slides, and other non-book materials. The rise of the computer and the development of a whole new technology of information, these prophets charge, will inevitably transform the role of the book in modern society.

It is ironic that the death or downgrading of the book should be debated seriously today. The American higher education community is in the midst of a library-building boom of unprecedented scope and thrust. According to the U. S. Office of Education, between 1958 and 1959, 52 new campus library structures rose at a cost estimated at $29,500,000. Between 1960 and 1961 another 69 new campus libraries sprang up at a cost of $38,650,000. And in the five-year period 1961-1965, fully 504 more libraries will come into being on college or university campuses at a cost of approximately $466,600,000. This means we are spending an annual average of over $93,000,000 on these new buildings designed to bring book and scholar together. These impressive figures do not include the cost of the books themselves, of salaries, or other operating expenses.

Why, at a time when the book is for the first time in history being challenged, are we pouring so much time, energy, and money into new libraries for our institutions of higher education? Campus libraries are overcrowded. Educators believe that college and university libraries should be able to seat anywhere from 25 to 50 per cent of the total enrollment of the institution at any given time. Yet the latest figures of the U. S. Department of Health, Education and Welfare paint a stark picture of shortages in capacity: "For the aggregate United States, as of December 31, 1957, the number of students who could be seated at one time in higher education library reading rooms represented 16.2 per cent of the fall 1957 enrollment." Construction since then has done little to narrow the gap. In fact, it may have widened since this report.

Behind the shortage of teaching capacity lies the powerful surge in student enrollment. And of the swelling wave of students descending on the colleges and universities, an increasing proportion go on to graduate study. According to Francis H. Horn, president of the University of Rhode Island, "They require much more service than do undergraduates. More space is needed....This means that libraries cannot be expected to provide for twice as many students in the future just by doubling present facilities, staffs, and appropriations." Furthermore, students at all levels are using libraries more than in the past. According to an announcement from Cornell University, "Students have been reading more books, too; during 1959-1960 a total of 873,903 books are recorded as having been used by Cornell students," not counting reference books. "This means that students at Cornell on the average are

consulting annually — in addition to their regular texts—more than 80 library books each—a stack of books from 12 to 15 feet high." By 1960-1961 the average had climbed further to 89 books per student.

An increase in library usage is reported almost everywhere. Says Stephen A. McCarthy, director of Cornell University Libraries: "This phenomenal rise in library use—steady over the last few years—apparently results from changes in teaching methods and from a greater sense of urgency and purpose on the part of the students." Henry James, assistant librarian at the Lamont Undergraduate Library at Harvard adds: "Today education is more sophisticated. Assignments are made not from a single book, but from many books, from government documents, pamphlets, journals, and magazine articles."

Meanwhile, another explosive force is at work. This is the accelerating growth in the number of books, journals, and other materials that libraries must house. The world has never known such a rapid proliferation of knowledge. In the words of the *Wall Street Journal*: "Every 24 hours enough technical papers are turned out around the globe to fill seven sets of the 24-volume *Encyclopedia Brittanica*. The output is rising every year. This year's crop: some 60,000,000 pages or the equivalent of about 465 man-years of steady round-the-clock reading." A more recent estimate by Charles P. Bourne of the Stanford Re-

search Institute put the number of significant journals being published around the world at 15,000, with perhaps 1,000,000 significant papers in them each year. These figures do not include books and other forms of publication. Information specialists say that the sheer quantity of information is doubling every 10 years.

The library that expects to serve its readers, and especially faculty researchers, must somehow attempt to keep up with this tidal wave of data. No library can store everything. But as intellectual disciplines subdivide into specialties and the relationships between disciplines multiply, collections must grow. The fantastic information explosion not only means that storage space must be expanded rapidly or some other means of storage developed, but that the costs of cataloging, clerical processing, and retrieving material are skyrocketing. Scholars, faculty researchers, and graduate students are drowning in a sea of data, and locating and obtaining any specific item of information is becoming harder and more time consuming.

Under such pressures the campus library is being transformed. The library of the University of Illinois Chicago Undergraduate Division, for example, will have to grow 1,000 per cent in less than 10 years, and is making preparations to do so. Cornell's new seven-story library, completed in 1960 at a cost of $5,700,000, houses 2,000,000 volumes, is cataloging new titles at the rate of 80,000 a year, and will be hard pressed for space again within 15 years.

At the same time, colleges and universities themselves are undergoing changes that must affect libraries. Colleges are becoming universities, meaning that their libraries must increase their collections to permit graduate research and more faculty use. Universities are broadening their scope to encompass new specialties. Moreover, educational philosophy itself is changing. As a result, according to Ralph Ellsworth, director of libraries for the University of Colorado, and a leading consultant on library construction: "Most libraries built before 1950 are either totally unusable or need to be remodeled or enlarged." The challenge confronting planners has never been so massive or so complex.

How may this challenge be met? How may the urgent demands of the present be confronted without compromising the future? How real is the threat to both book and library as we know them? To answer these and similar questions, it is necessary to cast a glance backward at the traditional library, at the upheaval that so recently replaced it, at the mood of library planners as they consolidate the gains of the past, and only then at the multiple possibilities of the future.

MONSIEUR LABROUSTE'S SKYSCRAPER

Libraries have been in existence at least since Assurbanipal, the Assyrian emperor of 2,500 years ago, kept a crew of copyists busy collecting and copying samples of the literature of his time. And builders have been worried about library design since the Roman Vitruvius urged that library rooms face east so that scholars might have the benefit of the morning sun as they bent over their scrolls. But the classic design of the library in modern times was established by a French architect, Henri Labrouste. M. Labrouste built a great library in Paris, the Bibliothèque Nationale, begun in 1858 and finished 10 years later. In doing so, he created a tradition that endured almost a century. The Bibliothèque Nationale was a monumental structure with vast, high-ceilinged reading rooms, elaborately decorated and covered with a huge dome. Inside it, M. Labrouste

constructed what was, in effect, a small skyscraper within a building—a five-story framework of cast iron columns and wrought iron beams—a gigantic rack to house the shelving for 900,000 volumes. Since this part, the stack, was closed to the public and not visible to outsiders, M. Labrouste felt free to do away with the ornamentation that covered the public spaces, and therefore to create a truly functional building within one that was not.

This same basic concept embracing two sharply differentiated parts, one grandly elaborate, the other Spartan in its simplicity, became the model for hundreds of libraries subsequently built elsewhere, and today monumental libraries, descendants of M. Labrouste's Bibliothèque, still dominate scores of American college and university campuses.

In these, as a rule, the section open to the public is an aggregate of reading or working rooms clustered around a central reading hall whose ceiling towers as much as 30 or 40 feet above the long tables and straight-backed chairs ranged below. Natural light filters in from windows set high above the floor. Huge marble stairways wind leisurely from floor to floor, and upstairs, somewhere near the top level, there may be small, book-lined seminar rooms in which groups of students can meet with their professors. Each room is set off from the others by thick, immovable, load-bearing walls. The stack area, either housed within the main building or in a separate annex con-

nected with the main building, consists of tier after tier of shelves, narrow staircases, and cramped aisles. Often floors are constructed of translucent glass tile so that light from a skylight in the roof may seep downward into the warehouse-like gloom.

While some of the monumental libraries that dot American campuses are, in their way, beautiful buildings, most were neither beautiful nor efficient from the beginning, and most are cripplingly inefficient today. Yet monumentalism reigned over the American campus right down through the 1930's. One after another, major new library buildings cropped up on university grounds, each a variation of the same basic theme. At Harvard, at Stanford, at Minnesota, Michigan, Illinois, and elsewhere the same lofty ceilings, impressive stairways, and ornamented walls turned up. Architects vied to make the buildings look imposing. To quote Ralph Ellsworth again, "The monumentality of a library was accepted as a symbolic measure of respect for knowledge in the minds of the university community."

The monumental library turned out to be hard to wire and light artificially, and almost impossible to heat and air condition efficiently. It was wasteful of space, too. As much as 25 per cent

Stacks of monumental Bibliothèque Nationale form skyscraper within a building. Designed in 1858, this building set the pattern for American campus libraries as late as the 1930's.

of its gross space was assigned to wide stairways, impressive lobbies, thick walls, and service facilities, leaving only 75 per cent for actual library functions. But its chief drawback was its rigidity. Each room or working space was designed to serve a single function and, set off by load-bearing walls, could be altered only with extreme difficulty. As functions changed with the passage of years, the rooms became increasingly inefficient.

This is illustrated by the change in the function of the stack. Throughout history, until fairly recently, the book (or the tablet or manuscript) was expensive and frequently rare. The library was primarily a repository, and the librarian's first impulse was to protect the collection from the reader. In the Middle Ages, books were chained to iron bars on library desks. In church libraries, monks wrote "book curses" into them to deter thieves. In our own country in 1667 the overseers of Harvard University ruled that "No schollar in the Colledge, under a Senior Sophister shall borrow a book out of the library." This air of possessiveness was reflected during M. Labrouste's time in the exclusion of readers from the stack.

By the 1920's, however, the whole philosophy of librarianship had begun to shift. Service to the reader became far more important than it had been. Books were cheaper, more easily available. On campuses, libraries came to be regarded less as passive repositories and more as an active part of the

teaching machinery. This new emphasis was reflected in a movement to throw the stack open to the student. Educators came to believe that there is positive intellectual value in encouraging the student to browse among thousands of books. By the 1920's the open, or at least partially open, stack had become commonplace among small- and medium-size libraries. The stack had thus become something more than just a place for storage.

This shift in the function of the stack dramatized the rigidity of the old monumental library. The tightly packed stack, created for maximum storage, lacked adequate aisle space for browsing. There was no handy place to set a table for readers to use near the shelves. Lighting and ventilation were inadequate for the increased traffic in the stack. Nor could the old-fashioned stack, designed to exclude rather than welcome people, be easily converted. The change in the philosophy of service created a conflict between function and form.

Similarly, as other concepts of librarianship changed with changing times, the frozen forms of the old monumental buildings stood more and more in the way of simple, efficient, and modern operation. Constricted by the walls around them, librarians took up the cry for more functional surroundings. During the 1930's the Depression slowed down the construction of new facilities. But by the early forties the attack on the monumental library had gained great force.

ENTER MR. MODULE

Ever since the mid-thirties Angus Snead Macdonald, a manufacturer of library shelving, had urged a radical change in library design. By 1943 he had built a mock-up of a completely new kind of library building. The contemporary library, Mr. Macdonald argued, should throw out the clichés of monumentalism. It should be built of light steel columns, beams, and panels. The columns should be hollow, providing vertical ducts for air conditioning. The cool air should flow into hollow chambers in the floors and be distributed into the rooms through registers in the ceilings. The ceilings, themselves, should be built to permit installation of flush lighting fixtures. And most important, each room should be set off, not by load-bearing walls, but by easily movable steel partitions.

Mr. Macdonald campaigned vigorously in articles and speeches for his idea of simple, wide-open spaces in libraries, broken only by impermanent walls that could be moved as functions in the library changed. Instead of thick walls to bear the weight of the upper stories, carefully distributed columns would do the job. The spaces bounded by these columns, i.e., the structural bays, were termed "modules," and Mr. Macdonald soon became known in the library profession as "Mr. Module," a tribute to his persistence and vigor.

Mr. Macdonald's ideas struck a responsive chord in Ralph Ellsworth, then librarian at the State University of Iowa. Dr. Ellsworth, a tall, husky, outspoken man, energetically proselytized for experimentation with Mr. Macdonald's ideas, and promptly began, with the backing of his institution, to build a so-called modular library at Iowa. The dominance of monumentalism came to an abrupt end.

The swiftness of the modular revolution was amazing. From the time Dr. Ellsworth built his new library at Iowa down to the present, hardly a single major campus library has been built in this country that has not, in one way or another, followed his lead. Few accepted every jot and tittle of Mr. Macdonald's mock-up. Even Dr. Ellsworth was unable to make use of the hollow columns. But free-flowing space became an article of faith in what can now be called the modular era. The modular library made possible an easy intermixture of reading spaces and stack spaces. The stack, instead of being structurally independent, was part of the building. Readers could move freely and comfortably through those stack areas open to them. The elimination of space-wasting stairways, thick walls, and elaborate decoration proved economical. Up to 85 per cent of gross space could actually be turned to true library use. Electrical outlets and ventilating ducts were easier to install and to alter. But most important of all, the modular plan made possible libraries that, in the words of one librarian, "you don't have to blow apart with dynamite to change."

The modular revolution affected almost every physical element of the building. The stack, the most rigid element of the traditional campus library, was transformed. In the traditional multi-tier stack, a series of vertical columns thrust up from the base to the top of the stack building. Floors were built around them, usually at intervals of about 7½ feet. The vertical columns were set in rows 3 feet apart, and the shelving actually hung on them so that all the weight was borne by these columns rather than the floors. The floors, in consequence, were relatively thin.

In the modular library the stacks are not structural elements at all. Instead, they consist of free-standing bookcases easily shifted from place to place. For standardization purposes they are still usually made in sections 3 feet long, but while the traditional stacks were made in rows set apart 4½ feet center to center, the aisle can now be made any desired width. Ordinarily, the 4½-foot width is still used, except where tables and other furniture are interspersed with bookcases. These dimensions, 3 by 4½, are often used to help determine the horizontal dimensions of the module or bay. Today architects strive to make the bay as large as possible in an effort to minimize the number of columns necessary and thereby enhance the easy convertibility of the space. Architect Gyo Obata, whose firm, Hellmuth, Obata and Kassabaum, is helping to create a new $25,000,000 campus for Southern

Illinois University at Edwardsville, Illinois, has designed a library that uses a 30 by 30 foot module, and at the University of Illinois at Chicago, architect Walter A. Netsch, Jr., of Skidmore, Owings and Merrill, has planned what is probably the largest module of any in the academic library field—30 by 45 feet.

One factor that limits the size of the module is floor strength. The further apart the columns are spaced, the stronger the floors have to be. This adds to cost. According to Mr. Obata, after a certain point, as the span widens, "You have to begin to do extra things like tensioning the reinforcing steel or using higher strength concrete to get the bigger span. The depth of your structural floor system gets much deeper, and you take on more height in the building." Just where the convenience of a larger bay warrants extra expenditure and where it does not is a point in hot dispute among architects and librarians, with most building planners leaning toward dimensions of 22½ feet or 27 feet.

As the bay or module expands, the floors tend to grow fatter. In modular buildings the books may be stored anywhere, and the floors must be able to carry a load of about 200 pounds per square foot. In addition, false ceilings are often hung beneath the structural floor leaving space above to accommodate ducts, wiring, and lighting fixtures. This, too, adds thickness. Some modern libraries have floors as thick as five feet. At Washington

University, whose new $3,000,000 library opened this fall, the architects, Murphy and Mackey, used flat slab concrete floors 9 inches thick, with drop ceilings hung from them only in certain parts of the building and not over the stacks.

The modular library concept also radically altered classical notions about the vertical space between floors—that is, room height. An adult can comfortably use a bookshelf that is about 7 feet tall. In traditional buildings, with the stack structure divided into stories roughly 7½ feet high, the surrounding reading rooms were frequently built so that their floors tied into certain stack floors. This meant that room heights were almost always multiples of the basic 7½-foot height of a single story in the stack. The lowest ceiling in a reading room was likely to be two stack levels high, or about 15 feet. The great reading hall, of course, was likely to be much taller. The consensus was that human beings are uncomfortable in rooms with low ceilings.

The modular library directly challenged this notion. According to Keyes D. Metcalf, Librarian Emeritus of Harvard and the dean of library construction consultants, the death knell of the high ceiling came when Princeton performed an unusual experiment. In preparing to build its own modular library, he says, "Princeton built a two-bay mock-up with a fake ceiling and cranked it up and down. They brought in librarians, students, architects, col-

lege presidents, faculty members, and others and asked them to holler when it got uncomfortable. They found the users could take it as low as 8'4" in a room as large as 25 by 36 feet." At Iowa, the library Dr. Ellsworth built has 8-foot ceilings. Today most modular libraries incorporate heights of about 8'6" for their reading areas.

The modular library brought with it air conditioning. The musty odor of the old-fashioned stack and the suffocating closeness of the cavernous reading room have been replaced by scientific comfort control. Libraries now being built are using air-conditioning equipment to accomplish a whole number of ends. First, temperature and humidity control make readers and staff comfortable all year round. Second, in many libraries, the air is electronically filtered to remove odors, smoke particles, and dust, thus reducing the time and money that must be spent cleaning the rooms and the collection. Many new libraries are "pressurized"—i.e., the air-conditioning level is such that when a door or window is opened air is forced out, thus keeping dirty or dusty air from rushing in. Third, the noise level of the system is so adjusted that it masks distracting sounds like the click of heels on tile, the clatter of a typewriter, or the opening and closing of doors. The air-conditioning system, in effect, maintains a comfortable backdrop noise. (Where the air-conditioning system has been set to operate too quietly, library users complain the building is noisy.)

The most important distinguishing characteristic of the modular library is the so-called loft space that is created by this type of design. Librarians are given great, wide-open spaces, whole floors broken only by a minimal number of fixed vertical elements. Architects, aware that any immovable vertical element constricts the librarian's freedom, have attempted to cluster the service areas in places where they get in the way of library functions as little as possible. In many libraries they are pushed outward toward the walls to leave the internal space clear. At Southern Illinois University this idea is to be carried one step further. Mr. Obata's plans call for pushing the service cores part way outside the walls. Thus, around the squarish three-story building rise six four-story towers. Each juts out from the walls of the building, rather than consuming space inside the walls. These house the elevator shafts, stairways, toilets, mechanical equipment, etc.

The modular revolution gave the librarian economy, efficiency, and a new sense of openness never before experienced. It also gave him the freedom to adapt his buildings to change.

THE HUMANIZATION OF THE MODULAR

Today the modular revolution, having triumphed, is in a new phase. The period of revolutionary zeal is over. A period of revision has begun—a period in which architects, librarians, consultants, and planners are rethinking their principles and applying them in new ways. Modularism is undergoing humanization.

When the modular revolution began, shortly after World War II, its critics charged that it would create large numbers of standardized, factory-like libraries across the country. Similar design principles had been used in the hasty construction of aircraft plants and similar structures during the war. Characteristically, they were long, low, unrelievedly bleak, and unimaginative. The loft spaces in them were too big, emphasizing the closeness of the ceilings and giving the interiors a claustrophobic appearance. The ruthless elimination of ornament heightened their look of grim, uninviting efficiency.

It is true that the modular revolution, like most revolutions, brought with it some excesses. A number of early modular libraries shared these unpleasant characteristics. But since the mid-fifties increasing attention has been paid to making college and university libraries livable.

What might be called the new humanism of the library can be seen in the way space is cut up and put together, as well as in the way it is subsequently furnished.

Inside the library, space must be set aside for a number of basic functions. Apart from the stack and the reading rooms, there must be space for a lobby, a centrally located card catalog, a reserve book room where students can come for assigned reading of books which are stocked in multiple copies by the library, a periodicals room, a reference room, a circulation counter and work space for the staff, receiving and shipping rooms, and work space for cataloging, mending, binding, ordering, or otherwise processing books.

Most new libraries now add to the basic areas listed above, special rooms for typing, for record listening, for seminars, small offices for faculty members engaged in research, conference rooms, lounges for student and staff, rare book rooms, exhibition spaces, and special lounges and study rooms for smokers. (Some libraries now permit smoking throughout and provide a few no-smoking rooms.) The Temple University library now being built in Philadelphia will even provide special study areas for blind students. Increasing attention to the needs of the individual rather than the mass is leading to increasing variety in space assignments.

This accent on the individual is reflected also in the growing importance now placed on providing private and semi-private study space for students. The large reading room of the past, with its long wooden tables and its institutional climate, is now being replaced by smaller rooms and alcoves, some formed by imaginative stack arrangements. According to Ralph Ellsworth: "It has been proven over and over again in college libraries that students don't like to read in large open

reading rooms. They like the privacy and the intimacy of small groups. They do not want to sit at flat tables in the middle of a large reading room."

This finding is strongly supported by the results of a survey conducted by four institutions, Amherst, Smith, Mt. Holyoke, and the University of Massachusetts. Nearly 400 students were polled on their preferences for certain types of study space. The results, in the words of the subsequent report, are a "challenge to the typical large library reading room. It may be economical in terms of the cost per student user, but it is expensive in terms of the quality of work done."

Just as the size of the reading room is growing smaller, more space is being devoted to individual seating, and especially to the use of carrels. (The study carrel is a small table with a raised partition on one, two, or three sides to screen off from the seated student visual distractions that interfere with concentration.) Says Keyes Metcalf, who planned the Lamont Undergraduate Library at Harvard and who has served as consultant to hundreds of other libraries around the world, "Since 1915 many libraries have provided large numbers of carrels for graduate students. Since 1949 we've had a great many individual seats in all parts of libraries, and I dared to put in up to 50 per cent individual seating when we were designing Lamont just after World War II. That was as far as I could go then. Today if it were done, I'd go to 75 or 80 per cent individual seating—and this for undergraduates." In university libraries, where many graduate students make use of the library, the proportion might even be higher. Carrels are often interspersed in or near the stack areas. At the just-opened Van Pelt Library of the University of Pennsylvania, individual work desks are built directly into the stack bookcases.

In many large libraries where long tables are still used, fewer students are placed at them. Thus at Washington University in St. Louis the large reading rooms are furnished with tables intended to seat eight, but only six chairs are ranged around them. At the beautiful new library of Colorado College, in Colorado Springs, the main reading room is furnished with small round tables for four.

This scaling down of space in the campus library for use by individuals or small groups rather than masses—this humanization of the modular library—has been accompanied by attempts to make the spaces themselves more inherently interesting and varied. Walter Netsch bluntly calls it "demodularization," and thinks it is a good thing. As he sees it, architects are now seeking to combine the beauties of the classical library with the efficiencies of the modular. "The classical idea of the dome is gone. But the new idea of the box is gone also," he says.

Behind this impulse toward modification of the box, Mr. Netsch says, is the need of mankind for a variety of space, rather than a uniformity of space. "You can have a world that's nine feet tall. It's technically feasible. ...But there is no universal space. Mankind needs different kinds of spaces for different kinds of activities."

Architect Obata expresses the need for variety and beauty in other terms: "Within the essentially horizontal spaces of the pure modular library we have very little chance to create any spaces that would add a new dimension for a person going through the building."

Ralph Ellsworth sees what is happening as less of a retreat from the modular than an advance in our ability to handle it. "We went through a period," he says, "when the architects took the modular idea and wrapped it up and put a cover around it. It's ugly. But now they are viewing the structure. They're learning how to use the medium, and some of the new modular libraries are extraordinarily beautiful."

One way in which architects are striving to regain the human element, the variety they find lacking in the unrelieved horizontality of the modular libraries, is through the creation of contrasting high-ceilinged spaces. At Washington University, designed by Murphy and Mackey, this takes the form of a small court that cuts through the building like an off-center hole in a donut and reaches up to open to the sky. This small square patio is moved off toward one corner of the large building so that it interferes little with the free space within. At Colorado College, a much smaller library achieves relief from the horizontal quality by creating a reading area that is two stories high with a mezzanine running around all four sides above it and a skylight roofing it over. This atrium is, indeed, a throwback to the high-ceilinged reading room of the past. But because it is in a small building, and is carefully furnished with small tables and groupings of lounge furniture, it avoids the institutional look. Its scale is human and intimate, its appearance warm and inviting.

This same concern for warmth and individuality is evident in the way in which new libraries are being outfitted. The old library, says Ellsworth Mason, librarian of Colorado College, speaking of his campus, "kept a lot of students out simply because it was totally unaesthetic and in a style that was dead as far as these kids were concerned. So we've paid very careful attention to appearance. The looks of a building influence very greatly whether or not the student wants to come in."

Today libraries are taking on some of the comfort of the home or of a well-furnished dormitory. The accent is on the provision of a variety of furniture forms so that each individual temperament can find some comfortable working space. As the four-college report on study habits declared: "Most institutional furniture is bought in standard sizes, but students don't come that way."

In consequence, libraries are getting away from the so-called standard

The modular and the human are blended in Colorado College library.

items and sizes. Here is what one architect, Theodore Wofford, of Murphy and Mackey, had to say about his firm's findings after building the new Washington University library and working on several others: "In a modular building the furniture becomes very important. We found that the traditional library suppliers had standard sizes, mostly geared to high-volume high school libraries, and much of it badly designed. So we gambled and went to high-quality furniture houses. Working with the library staff, we programed each piece of furniture for them, giving them the size, its purposes, etc., and asked them if they would be interested in a no-strings-attached arrangement to develop designs to meet our requirements. Many did. And so did some of the regular library suppliers.

"This took two years. We worked with Knoll, Herman Miller, Jens Risom, Dunbar, Steelcase, General Fireproofing, and others, including Art Metal and Remington Rand. Some of the houses came up with a full line of designs. The fine furniture houses are increasingly aware of the volume of library building and are eyeing this market. This whole process paid off. We took the best furniture we could afford, and we feel we have a more attractive and comfortable library than we might have gotten by doing things the standard way."

Fabric or leather-covered armchairs, coffee tables, couches, and table lamps turn up with increasing frequency in alcoves, lounges, or lobbies of the humanized library. In the study rooms a variety of carrels are being tried out, offering different kinds of partitions, some with shelves for storing books, others with extra large surfaces, some made of wood panels, others of various kinds of peg board or composition. Says Walter Netsch: "We need to do more research on the efficiency of different kinds of study room furniture. Aside from the standard carrel, consideration should also be given to the old-fashioned stand-up carrel. Maybe some people like to work that way. Remember Thomas Wolfe wrote standing up. And how about the big over-sized tablet arm that Ben Franklin had on his chair. We need maximum variety."

The concern for comfort is also more and more evident to anyone who looks downward in a library. Carpets, once unknown in the library, and bitterly opposed by maintenance people, are now turning up as a pleasant, efficient, and economical addition to modern campus libraries. "A reference librarian walks eight miles a day," says Colorado's Mr. Mason, "and our beautiful carpeting is wonderful for the staff. But the kids love it, too. They will sit down in front of a stack right on the floor to browse through a low shelf. I find myself doing it!"

Says architect Eugene Mackey, "There's been a terrific breakthrough in carpeting, on price as well as in the kinds there are—acrilan, nylon, dacron—and others. And you can use them to provide color."

A cost analysis drawn up for the John Crerar Library at Illinois Institute of Technology shows the comparative costs of carpeting, cork tile, vinyl asbestos tile, homogeneous vinyl tile, and asphalt tile. Initial costs for carpeting are still higher than for any of the other kinds of floor covering included. But maintenance costs are significantly lower, and the most expensive grade of carpeting analyzed in the study turned out to be cheaper to own and maintain than all other types of covering in less than 8 years. The carpeting was given a life expectancy of 15 years.

Carpeted, colorful, and quiet, tastefully designed and decorated, offering a variety of spaces and furnishings for its users, the humanized modular library of today is a far cry from the rather formal, artificially hushed, poorly ventilated, and dimly lighted library of the not-too-distant past.

THE STUPIDEST MONK PROBLEM

Hundreds of years ago Leibnitz predicted that, "If the world goes on this way for a thousand years and as many books are written as today, I am afraid that whole cities will be made up of libraries." Today more books are being written than ever and although no city has yet been drowned under a sea of paper, thoughtful librarians have long been pondering whether libraries must—or can—continue to increase the size of their collections *ad infinitum.* The increase is swelling both the size and the cost of campus libraries.

A growing body of opinion holds that librarians must get over the traditional idea that the bigger the collection, the better the library. Perhaps the most vociferous critic of the size of libraries today is Mortimer Taube, a former librarian, now chairman of the board of a company called Documentation, Inc. "Libraries are too big today," Mr. Taube charges. "The question is how much of the total past are you going to embalm? The stupidest book written by the stupidest monk in the Middle Ages is a rarity today. We want to own it, not because it contains useful information but because it's a historical artifact. This attempt to embalm the living past is silly. Why, we're worse than the ancient Egyptians. We're trying to mummify the past. An enormous number of the books collected today are not collected as books at all. Nobody wants to read them. They are collected because their very existence is presumed to tell us something about the society that produced them. Is this the job of the library? And how many copies of each one do we need?"

To date no way has been found to stem the ever swelling tide of material that is finding its way into campus collections. But a number of positive steps have been taken. Libraries have begun serious programs aimed at weeding out insignificant items from their collections, and determining use patterns for the books and other materials they own.

Libraries are also banding together to carry out two other programs to help alleviate the problem of mushrooming collections. First, groups of libraries are linking up to create regional storage warehouses for their least-used materials. Thus there are today three interlibrary storage centers. The Mid-West Interlibrary Center in Chicago serves about 20 libraries from Kansas to Minnesota and Ohio; the Hampshire Interlibrary Center services Amherst, Smith, the University of Massachusetts, and Mt. Holyoke; and the New England center handles overflow from a dozen libraries in the Boston area, including Harvard, Tufts, and the Massachusetts Institute of Technology.

But putting books into storage is clearly not a final solution to the problem. While it is cheaper to store materials in warehouse space than in library space, there is a limit, too, to how much storage is practical. Says Mortimer Taube with a snort: "Dead storage is like making four copies of everything before you throw it away."

The second and more imaginative interlibrary program is designed to restrict the size of collections by birth control rather than *ex post facto* means. Called the Farmington Plan, this program brings together some 60 libraries into a systematic division of labor. Each participant is given responsibility for building its collection in a special field of knowledge. Thus Cornell has the nation's best collection of Icelandic literature; Harvard has the best collections in philosophy and law; Princeton's chief specialty is mathematics; and the University of Minnesota boasts the best Scandinavian collection. Each institution buys the periodicals in its own field, and goes lightly in other fields. In this way the nation's campuses can support first-rate collections without heavily duplicating one another's activity. All collections are recorded in the National Union Catalog so that scholars can locate their materials through a central clearinghouse.

Another step being taken by campus librarians to keep their expanding collections under control is called compact storage. Here, certain materials are stored in big drawers jammed full. They take up less space than they would if ranged on shelves in the normal manner. Though they are cumbersome to handle, some libraries find this eminently practical for books and other materials that are called for infrequently.

But the most important and most promising steps to control the physical size of collections have to do with microreproduction, that is, the reduction of the materials to diminutive size. The best-known technique for doing this is, of course, microfilm. Here, the pages of periodicals or books may be reduced to fingernail size on strips of film. These, when needed, are fed through reading machines which

enlarge the image and convert it to black on white. Microfilm techniques are hardly new, but they are being used more widely than ever before. One reason for this is the availability of more and more material in this form. At St. Louis University, for example, scholars have access to 600,-000 manuscripts, including histories, biographies, chronicles, annals, notes, and other documents from the famed Vatican Manuscript Library. Between 1953 and 1955 crews of technicians shot 873,000 feet of film in the Vatican to compress 11,000,000 manuscript pages into manageable proportions, and thereby, with the permission of the Vatican, brought to the United States one of the world's great collections of the history of theology, philosophy, the church, and Renaissance humanism.

Today the librarian can also use similar techniques to compress collections. Microreproductions are available on index cards—microcards—and in other shapes and sizes. These techniques are regarded as especially important today when all libraries face the problem of book embrittlement. Recent studies have shown that much of the book paper produced since the turn of the century is subject to rapid deterioration. A recent test revealed that, of 400 books manufactured between 1900 and 1939, the paper in 89 per cent of them had a fold strength less than that of newsprint. What this means is that the sheer passage of time will, before too many decades, literally

destroy vast sections of present book collections. Microreproduction is looked to as a way of saving some of these doomed materials.

However, microreproduction techniques are not a panacea for the problem of sprawling collections. First, the need for a machine of some kind to enlarge the images means that users do not have the physical freedom that book users enjoy. The Council on Library Resources is supporting studies aimed at developing a simple, lightweight, and effective pocket reader — an enlarging lens and bracket of some kind that readers can carry with them anywhere. But there are a number of prickly optical problems to be solved before this can be accomplished. Secondly, many readers, especially researchers, need the convenience of a book. Study through a reading enlarger makes it difficult to flip through pages, to scan, or to browse for material. The machines often must be used in subdued light.

It is, of course, now possible to have photographic enlargements made of each frame of the microreproduction, but this is still a fairly costly and time-consuming method. However, Univer-

sity Microfilms, Inc., in Ann Arbor, Michigan, has started a service through which Xerox copies, in paperbound form, of microfilmed books can be obtained at 3½ cents a page. Copies of doctoral dissertations run slightly higher — 4½ cents a page. But the service is limited to the firm's existing microfilm collection: 15,000 books printed in English prior to 1640, 6,000 out-of-print books, and 50,000 doctoral dissertations.

From the point of view of the library planner, too, microreproduction is less advantageous than might seem at first blush. While the compression of collection material into diminutive form is, of course, a great space saver, the reading machines require space. As a result, until a library has a fairly large collection in microform, it is not likely to save much in square footage.

According to Verner W. Clapp, president of the Council on Library Resources: "Microfilm will enrich collections, not replace them. It is possible to make microfilm almost as convenient as books. But we haven't done it yet. At present it's downright abominable." Nevertheless, it is predictable that more and more use will be made of microreproduction in years to come. It is a sign of the times that the Mormon Geneological Society in Salt Lake City is building a reading room that will house 750 reading machines. The switchover to microfilm was partially responsible for a decision to abandon plans for a 15-story archives building to house the Society's records.

THE WIRED-IN STUDENT

The day is thus long past when libraries stored books alone. In addition to microform material, all new libraries now must make provision for new forms of material like phonograph records, tapes, films, slides, even, in some cases, kinescopes, and, of course, the machines needed to make use of these information carriers. Apart from special racks and storage facilities, and in some cases, special catalogs, the introduction of audio-visual equipment often brings with it the need for special areas in which it may be used. With instructors assigning spoken word LP records to their classes, so that the student may hear T. S. Eliot reading his own poetry or John Gielgud doing Hamlet, the listening booth or earphones have become commonplace in the campus library. Rooms are also set aside for the projection of movies, filmstrips, and slides.

The tape recorder is cropping up with ever greater frequency in college libraries, and the library stocks taped lectures, foreign language lessons, and similar material. In some libraries tape recorders are installed in booths or carrels. In others the student may pick up a portable unit at the reserve desk and carry it to a place set aside for listening. At Washington University a room has been set aside for mobile tape recorder units into which a number of students simultaneously may plug their earsets. With ever greater emphasis being placed on educational television, libraries are also equipping themselves for closed-circuit reception.

Another form of material that may be expected to become important in campus libraries is the teaching machine program. Librarians are talking about the day when teaching machines will be signed out as books are now.

Perhaps the most ambitious project presently in the development stage is the so-called environmental carrel. Unlike the traditional carrel which is nothing much more than a small table partially enclosed by partitions, the environmental carrel would be equipped to receive information electronically in a number of forms, and to dial out for the data needed.

Sol Cornberg, former director of studio and plant planning for the National Broadcasting Company and now head of his own firm of "designers in the communication arts," has been engaged by Grand Valley State College, a new institution near Grand Rapids, Michigan, to install the most up-to-date audio-visual equipment possible. The library now being built there will contain 256 carrels, each outfitted with a microphone, two loudspeakers, an eight-inch TV picture tube, and a telephone dial. As Mr. Cornberg describes it: "Any information stored in a 'use attitude' will be available to the student. There will be up to 310 audiotapes—that is, 310 talking books. These will be programed for self-learning. On a typical day the student would go to his class or laboratory. That is, he would participate in a group learning activity. After his lesson he goes to his carrel for individual learning. There, by simply dialing a code number, he will be able to get a repeat of the lecture, excerpts as they apply to his assigned lesson, a list of problems. He will use the microphone to record his answers on tape, erase and correct them, if necessary, then dial his instructor. He then plays the tape for the instructor."

The advantage of this system, Mr. Cornberg says, "is that it presents a controlled environment. The student works at his own pace. There is no problem of being too shy to raise one's hand or too exhibitionistic and, therefore, a disruptive influence in the class. It's a more objective learning situation."

Such carrels could, in theory, be placed anywhere on the campus, not only in the library. But even if they were not housed in the library, the library would have the responsibility for storing the tapes, videotapes, films, and other materials. A similar system is envisioned as being part of the new library now planned at Stephens College in Columbia, Missouri. So far, it must be cautioned, no such fully equipped carrel has been placed in actual operation anywhere, but the technical problems of producing them are not overwhelming. Their usefulness, of course, will depend largely on how much information will be stored "in a use attitude"—that is, how much will be available in the appropriate forms and how much of that will be properly coded for remote dialing.

With the development of such mechanical teaching aids still in its infancy, it is impossible to predict just how deeply they will affect campus libraries. But already the audio-visual invasion has created design problems for academic libraries. The biggest and most important of these is whether, in fact, the entire audio-visual function should be a part of the library. At the Southern Illinois University, where this question was thoroughly explored, the decision reached was that a separate "communications building" right next door to the library should house TV production studios and all audio-visual materials. "We felt it was developing so fast that it was important to put it in a separate building," says Mr. Obata. At Stephens College, a pioneer in the use of closed-circuit TV for teaching, the decision of the architects and planners again was that a special building was needed. "We started out to put all the audio-visual into the library," says Joseph Murphy of Murphy and Mackey, the architects. "We ended up finding that this was not as practical as it seemed. While the user in the library still has access to a full range of audio-visual resources, it was more sensible and economical to put the TV production and the master control facilities in a separate building. What we had was not a group of flexible spaces, but a group of specialized spaces and equipment that required studios and office space, and eventually needed a whole building."

In contrast, there are strong arguments for including audio-visual centers in library buildings. One is that libraries are equipped to acquire, process, and catalog the materials needed. Another argument is put forward by Keyes Metcalf, who points out that "We tend to build libraries about twice as large as they are needed at the time of construction because libraries double their collections in 16 years. This means that for the first few years you have extra space in the library. We have no idea how far audio-visual can go in the next few years, and it is therefore foolish to put up audio-visual buildings as such. The new library can give it space for the next 5 years, until we know more about how far it will go in higher education."

This fundamental policy question has not been decided by campus planners yet. It is likely to arouse heated controversy in the next few years.

FROM CLAY TABLET TO PUSH BUTTON

Reading machines, teaching machines, electronic carrels, closed-circuit television, tape recorders, motion-picture screens—the age of technology is moving into the hitherto machineless quiet of the library. At one end of the historical spectrum, a slave carving a message in a clay tablet; at the other, a whirring, computerized push-button library. Today, after nearly 3,000 years of development, the library is just now entering the machine age, and the possibilities are so cloudy and complex that no one can say with assurance how fast or how far the mechanization or automation of the library will travel in the foreseeable future. Nevertheless, for those faced with the need to finance or plan new campus libraries no issue is more significant, and even an educated guess about the future is better than none. Today librarians and architects are trying to piece together just such an educated guess. It seems inevitable that the campus library will make far greater use of machines than ever before. But for what purposes? To what end? How soon? And in what ways?

One relatively simple way in which the age of technology will make itself felt in libraries will be through the mechanization of certain clerical processes that now occupy increasing staff time in any medium or large campus library. According to Donald V. Black, director, Library Operations Survey, University of California at Los Angeles, "A lot of libraries have come to the point in their history at which they're being asked embarrassing questions. Administrations are beginning to cast a rather jaundiced eye at the vast sums of money going into operating costs."

How high these costs can run is indicated by the fact that cataloging, preparing, and shelving a new book routinely costs more than twice the price of the book itself in many libraries. One recent study put the price of book processing at between $10 and $15 per volume. It is now believed that automation can not only speed the paperwork of the library, but cut processing costs as well. In Don Black's words: "Here we have a situation very much resembling ordinary business. Take circulation records. In circulation we have something very much like inventory control. In acquisition work we get invoices from a dealer, we approve them for payment, we process them in some way, and send them on to the comptroller's office to write checks. Straightforward business. Has nothing to do with libraries except the fact that the materials we are buying are library materials. Many businesses automated this kind of activity years ago."

In acquisitions work, libraries first must review the catalogs and other advertising materials submitted to them by publishers and dealers. Selections are made. Then the existing collection must be searched to determine whether or not the items to be purchased are already owned. This is sometimes tricky because the same work may appear several years later under a new title, or as part of some other volume. Large libraries today spend thousands of dollars continually searching dealers' offers and then matching them against their collections. Campus libraries often get faculty members to help make selections. But even with this help, large staffs are required just to execute the acquisitions function.

At the University of Missouri, whose librarian, Ralph Parker, has for years urged the mechanization of routine library functions, a sophisticated IBM punch card system helps cut acquisition costs. Once an item is definitely selected for purchase, an IBM card is punched for it. This card indicates the author, title, publisher, date of publication, edition, number of copies wanted, the account from which the funds are to be drawn, the dealer from whom it is to be purchased, and several other facts. The cards are machine sorted by dealer, then fed into a Cardatype machine which actually types out the order form. The cards are then re-sorted according to the account from which funds are to be drawn, and they are used to update the ledger automatically. The University of Florida library operates in similar fashion and, according to Mr. Parker, his system has brought a stream of visitors to the campus.

At the University of Colorado, IBM punch cards are used for ordering and bookkeeping, and the university is taking the lead in setting up an integrated purchasing system for all seven state-supported college and university libraries in Colorado.

A related library activity that also lends itself to automation is "serials control." This is the process of keeping tabs on which issues of periodicals arrive at the library. This sounds easy enough but, as Verner Clapp of the Council on Library Resources explains: "This is one of the messy operations in a library. The Library of Congress, for example, acquires 100,-000 separate serials (i.e., periodicals)

and employs 40 people just in recording them. Harvard has 28. And even so, records are unsatisfactory. This ought to be automated. It's just checking and matching. It's dumb-cluck stuff."

Yet developing a system for serials control that covers thousands of different publications issued at different rates of frequency, arriving from different sources, and printed in dozens of languages, is not simple. At the University of California, San Diego, librarian Melvin Voigt is working to crack this problem with a computer. Mr. Voigt is now able to keep tabs on 800 English and foreign titles by computer, and hopes, by the end of 1963, to boost the number to 3,000 titles. No total cost figures are available yet, but Mr. Voigt is confident that serials control by computer will prove to be economical. "Should Mr. Voigt demonstrate that he can beat the costs of doing it by hand, this application of the machine might be embraced by 100 universities tomorrow," Mr. Clapp believes.

Acquisitions and serials control involve incoming material. Circulation control involves outgoing books and materials. Just how massive a job this is can be gauged from the following statistics from the University of Illinois, Chicago Undergraduate Division Library—not one of the largest by any means. This library handles 400,000 circulations a year, sends out 30,000 to 35,000 overdue notices, plus an additional 3,000 to 9,000 faculty notices. It has been estimated that this entire

record keeping job could be done by a computer operating just six minutes a day. Mr. Parker at the University of Missouri has been using punch cards to keep circulation records, and he is now at work developing an integrated system that will knit together into a single process both acquisitions and circulation control. In the process of recording the purchase order a card will be punched for each title. This card will be inserted in the pocket of the book when it arrives at the library and is shelved. In addition, each borrower will carry an identification card. At the check-out desk the borrower's card and the book card will be inserted in a machine to produce a so-called transaction card. From transaction cards it will be possible to create for each book a complete case history from the time it is ordered to the time it is finally withdrawn from inventory.

Such a system will provide not only the records needed to control circulation and acquisition, but a stream of operational statistics that will help Mr. Parker run a more efficient library. The system will kick out answers to questions like: How much duplication of material is there in the library? What type of material is being duplicated? What proportion of the collection is in languages other than English? How much are these used? Mr. Parker estimates that his present punch card equipment is saving him between $8,000 and $10,000 a year in direct, calculable dollars. But the "operations analysis" the system makes possible creates additional savings elsewhere and, he notes, he is able to eliminate significant waste by freeing his professional staff from routine drudge work and applying their talents to more productive activities.

The time has now come, Mr. Parker believes, for his library to convert from punch card operation to computer, and he is exploring the applicability of the IBM Ramac. Computerization would eliminate much of the slow and clumsy manual manipulation of the cards, he says, and would speed up the entire process. It would also make it possible to avoid peak work loads. "For instance," he explains, "at the end of the fiscal year, when we run out of money, we traditionally hold back orders until after July 1, and after that we're swamped with work. With the speed of the computer we can go ahead and prepare much of the work in advance."

The circulation activity would be improved, too. The borrower would present his identification card and the book to be borrowed at the desk. The two cards would be inserted in a machine at the counter. In less than three seconds the transaction would be completed and the borrower on his way. At the end of the day all the transactions, both lending and return, would be fed into the computer which will maintain in its "memory" a record, not only of every book outstanding, but of every borrower. The Ramac, renting for $2,600 a month, would considerably reduce the need for people at the loan desk, and would be capable of handling all the work now being done by punch cards. Mr. Parker estimates he will be ready for his computer within two or three years.

The computer is only economical after a certain scale of operation is reached. According to Don Black, who has researched the potentials of computer operation for U.C.L.A., "if we could link these three functions—acquisitions, serials control, and circulation—into a single system for computer, which I believe is perfectly possible, then we could easily justify the cost of the computer. We would replace enough personnel and handle enough increased volume to pay for it, and probably save money to boot. Just within the circulation operation alone we believe we're going to save $8,000 a year right now, net. When an institution gets above 10,000 students, and has a book purchase budget of around $150,000 a year, and a collection of 300,000 or 400,000 titles, it has reached the point at which it warrants a small-scale computer exclusively for clerical processing."

Just what impact the coming mechanization of clerical processing will have on the design of new library buildings is still problematical. It is apparent that different interior arrangements of work space will be required for conducting the paper work of the library. The circulation desk, the acquisitions area, and the serials control space, will all probably be smaller in the future than they are now. But space will have to be provided for some of the machines themselves. More than this it is, at present, impossible to predict.

THE CASE OF THE $5,000 FILE DRAWERS

At the same time that clerical processing in the library is being automated or mechanized, steps are being taken to harness the machine for far more complex library functions. The second point of attack, one already receiving considerable attention from researchers, is the library catalog, a central determinant of the interior layout of libraries today.

The catalog, consisting of hundreds of drawers of index cards listing the books of the library by author, title, and subject matter, and located in a central place in the library, represents the key to the collection. The user, after finding the appropriate card in the catalog, reads from it the number assigned to the book he seeks. This number is, in effect, the address of the book, a code indicating its location in the stack. The catalog is an essential part of any library; it is also, librarians believe, a barrier between the user and his material. As one librarian puts it: "Particularly in large libraries the catalog becomes a mammoth thing, a monster almost."

The larger the collection grows, the more unwieldy the catalog. In big libraries whole crews of catalogers are kept busy assigning numbers to new titles and filing cards for them in the catalog drawers. As the drawers fill up, new sections must be added and the cards redistributed, a job that requires months of advance planning and weeks of work to accomplish. Moreover, as the catalog expands, the time and cost of filing each new card increases. "We believe on the basis of some studies that catalogers spend 90 per cent of their time moving back and forth between their desks and the catalog and thumbing through cards," says Donald Black. "The intellectual part of their work occupies only 10 per cent of their time. Yet catalogers are in short supply, and they are among the highest paid library workers."

The card catalog, representing a fantastic concentration of labor, time, and money, is a one-of-a-kind proposition. It is the central control of the library, and no duplicate of it exists. There is no reference point to check back against when something goes wrong with it. Thus at U.C.L.A., when four catalog drawers were stolen some time back (presumably by a prankster) the job of reconstituting those drawers took on prodigious proportions. Deducing what cards had been in them, searching the miles of stack shelving for clues, and making up and filing a new set of cards ran to an estimated $20,000 in expense—$5,000 a drawer.

The catalog is also highly expensive to house. The cases in which it is filed are usually the single largest item of

cost in the furniture and equipment budget, apart from the stacks. It is estimated that these cases cost one cent per card. This means that for a library with 1,000,000 volumes, each requiring about four cards in the catalog, the cases alone run to roughly $40,000. A catalog of this size would occupy, perhaps, 1,500 square feet of choice, central space in the building, which, if it cost $25.00 a square foot would represent a capital expenditure of $37,500. In short, the catalog is to the library what the memory is to the mind. And its costs are commensurate with its importance.

From the point of view of cost, then, as well as from the point of view of making life easier for the library user, who is often intimidated by the sheer bulk and complexity of the catalog, anything that can be done to streamline the catalog is worth doing. Several things can be done—either now or in the foreseeable future.

One approach is described by Don Black: "You could put the catalog in a computer memory. This would be difficult and costly, but not impossible. You could then hook into this storage unit a number of what are called input-output stations. These are devices with a small television screen and a keyboard. The user looking, say, for a copy of 'Information and Communication in Biological Science' by Lowell Hattery, punches in the author and title on his keyboard. The computer is activated. It searches its memory, prints out the call number of the book,

and transmits it to the station via television. You could put these stations—which, incidentally, only cost about $800 apiece—not only in the library but in each of the department offices, even in dorms."

Such a system, Mr. Black estimates, could go into operation for an expenditure of about $30,000 for equipment plus a monthly rental of about $2,-400. In addition to this it would take about $20,000 to translate his catalog's 3,000,000 cards into readable language for the machine and feed it into the memory unit. These figures do not include, however, the unascertainable cost of developing the programs necessary to instruct the computer how to respond to queries. This would quite likely cost far more than the $20,000 for simply preparing the catalog and programing is by no means easy.

Nevertheless, an ambitious yearlong project recently completed by librarians of the University of Illinois at Chicago, working with experts provided by manufacturers of data processing equipment, now shows the way not merely to automate the catalog, but to go beyond this and link cataloging with clerical processing functions in a single, overarching computer system that could revolutionize the field.

This system would begin with the punching of IBM cards for each new title to be purchased. These cards would be fed into a computer and the information from them stored in a magnetic tape storage unit. The computer would be programed to print out the actual order form to be sent to the publisher or book dealer, then to deduct automatically the necessary funds from the appropriate source. At this point the machine would create a weekly list of titles "in process." Once a month the machine would print out a cumulative list of new titles that have already arrived.

At the same time the entire catalog of the library's holdings would be fed into the machine, which in turn would print out a holdings catalog in book form. Duplicate copies of this book could, like the input-output stations mentioned above, be distributed around the campus at convenient places so that a student or researcher could actually do a good deal of his bibliographic research without setting foot in the library building itself. (Users could determine the catalog number of the books they want and phone the library. A messenger service would be provided to deliver the books to them.) At intervals the cumulative new titles catalog and the main catalog would both be run through the machine to create a single up-to-date book catalog, with as many duplicate copies as are needed. The loss of a drawerful of cards would no longer be a disaster.

The computer would also create a daily list of books out on loan, and automatically print out overdue notices when necessary. Developers of this system also plan to produce magnetic tape units that store lists of faculty reading interests. These tapes would be automatically matched with titles of incoming books, and notices would be printed alerting faculty members of the arrival of new volumes in which they may have an interest. The system, its developers believe, can also be extended to carry out serials processing.

The effect of such a system on the physical layout of the library building has yet to be determined. But at present the positioning of the card catalog dictates many other interior design decisions. This is true because it must be conveniently available to users, to catalogers, to reference librarians, and others. The reduction of the catalog to tapes or discs inside a computer storage unit, and the distribution of books or input-output stations around the campus would open up many possibilities for new and varied uses of space in the library building and for possible reductions in the space needed.

THE LIBRARY OF THE FUTURE

Such developments and others, like the preparation of *Index Medicus,* an index of medical literature prepared through sophisticated machine techniques by the National Library of Medicine, all represent milestones on the path to the push-button library. By most of those who use the term, this is taken to mean a library based on a fully automatic information retrieval system. In such a library the user would rely on machines not only to tell him where to locate the book or journal article he wants, but literally to deliver to him its contents. If card catalogs can be fed into a computer memory, why can't the data now stored in books? Indeed, say many critics of the *status quo,* unless some way is found to crack this problem, data recovery will become so time consuming and costly as collections swell in size in the future, that research will grind slowly to a halt.

As a result, an intensive effort to solve the technical and intellectual problems associated with automatic information retrieval is now under way around the world. Researchers, technicians, scholars, librarians, and others are at work, not merely in the United States, but in Japan, India, Belgium, Holland, France, England, and other nations, on the host of mechanical and related problems that still bar the way to the library of the future. Information retrieval, mechanical translation, automatic indexing and classifying, optical scanning or pattern recognition, high speed photography, and printing, are a few of the subjects being probed. Much of this research is financed by military and intelligence agencies, but its potential impact on libraries is profound.

Out of this melange of research two main lines of attack emerge. In one, the actual documents—pages of books, for example — would be reduced by microreproduction techniques to pinhead size, then stored on film in what is, in effect, an information warehouse — a miniature library. Each item is coded, and a memory unit in a computer "remembers" where it is located in the warehouse. One version of this system (there are several) has been produced by IBM for the Central Intelligence Agency, and is known as WALNUT. The WALNUT system makes it possible to recover any of millions of documents or book pages within five seconds. The user starts his search by writing a few key words on a form. These might be "library," "technology," and "computer." From this form a punched tape is made, and this directs the computer to search its memory for headings related to these key words. The machine then presents the user with a list of documents relevant to his study. He indicates which he wants.

When he does, the computer locates the item and activates a mechanical device that extracts the appropriate film. The images on this film may then be enlarged and read on a viewer, or may be photographically enlarged and converted into so-called hard copy— i.e., a duplicate of the printed original.

The second line of attack condenses the information itself, not merely its physical embodiment. The ideal system based on this principle would begin with a scanning device which automatically "reads" printed matter and translates it into machine language. Next the material is abstracted, classified, and indexed auto-matically and stored in a computer. The user can call up relevant abstracts automatically, but he goes about getting the original documents he may want in the conventional manner. He is spared reading in full a lot of material that he doesn't really need, and the machine sharply reduces the amount of time he needs to spend searching.

Primitive systems employing both methods now exist, although most have only a relatively small capacity for data storage. Which line of research will prove the most practical and economical in the years ahead is impossible to predict with assurance. In either case, the concentrated study of the entire problem, and the growth of what might be called information science, will necessarily reshape the library.

One form that the library of the future may take has been sketched dramatically by John D. Kemeny, chairman of the Department of Mathematics at Dartmouth, in a paper read as part of the Massachusetts Institute of Technology Centennial Lecture Series. Speaking of the continuing growth of Brobdingnagian collections, Dr. Kemeny talks of the day when libraries could reach the 100,000,000 volume mark. "It is clear," he states, "that the cost of building, of purchasing volumes, of cataloging, and of servicing these monstrous libraries will ruin even our richest universities."

The only solution to the problem of mushrooming magnitude, Dr. Kemeny believes, is the creation of a national research library big enough to hold the equivalent of 300,000,000 volumes in miniaturized form. He proposes storing all this data on film tapes retrievable by computer. The user could have access to this central storage center without leaving his campus, through the help of a multi-channel cable on which data can be transmitted. "The university," says Dr. Kemeny, "will have a large number of reading units scattered around the campus, some at the university library, some in departmental reading rooms, and some in individual professors' offices"—the number to depend on the institution's size and "library" budget.

These reading machines would have within them "reading tapes" similar to Videotape, a three-inch section of which, he calculates, could hold the equivalent of 10 miniaturized volumes. The reader would dial a number to be connected with the central storage bank. From it the relevant tape would be extracted, and an image of its contents transmitted through the cable to the user's reading machine. These images would be reproduced on the strip of reading tape inside the reading machines. The reading tape could then be projected on the reading machine's screen, much as microfilm is today, or it could be photographically enlarged to make a full-scale duplicate of the original book or document.

It has been suggested that instead of a single central information storage bank, regional centers might be established at different universities, each perhaps specializing in certain fields of knowledge as the participants in the Farmington Plan already do.

Dr. Kemeny, who speaks of this centralized information bank as "the library of 2000 A.D.," does not believe that such massive information centers would necessarily do away with campus libraries, but they would, of necessity, radically transform their functions. He says, "I take it for granted that our university libraries will *not* be abolished, even if their role becomes secondary. Partly this will be due to the fact they will serve a limited but useful purpose, but mainly to the fact that faculty members will be reluctant to give up personal contact with books." In this connection, Dr. Kemeny urged retention on the campus of any book that might be consulted as often as once a week. This would include, he said, "present reference rooms, as well as core research libraries in all subjects. The periodicals room would still serve as useful a purpose as in the past . . . Students would have books on reserve . . ." But all of these functions, Dr. Kemeny declared, "could be fulfilled comfortably with a collection of no more than a few hundred thousand volumes," and this, he added, was a generous estimate. These small libraries might be permitted to grow slowly, but a ruthless control over their size would be exercised, and the spaces now used as libraries, but freed by automation, could be converted to faculty studies and reading

rooms, in the sense indicated above—that is, rooms with receiving machines.

There are, however, those who go even further than Dr. Kemeny in predicting the contraction of the campus library. According to Sol Cornberg, perhaps the most radical prophet of the new library technology, the campus library is doomed. Books, says Mr. Cornberg, "are inefficient. It's not that we don't like them—my wife is a novelist, as a matter of fact—but they just aren't the best way to transmit information anymore. We don't like the laborious problems of finding information in them. Furthermore, to serve a thousand students you need multiple copies. You need storage space for them. The weight of the books is reflected in the architectural costs. Floors get heavier, steel supports, foundations get heavier. Yet in a cabinet the size of my desk or a bit higher we can store 20,000 volumes on microfilm. Nobody can tear a page out of them. They don't smell of old vellum or glue, but you can browse through them and sit there and read them."

Mr. Cornberg goes further. The day when reading will be a primary form of information intake is also passing, he believes. Students will learn better and faster through audio-visual techniques, with films, lectures, and other materials piped directly to them in their homes. "Reading and writing will become obsolete skills," he predicts.

At Grand Valley State College, where Mr. Cornberg is installing the

latest audio-visual equipment, he conducted a successful battle to restrict the size of the library to no more than 23,000 volumes. Even this many books he considers a concession to the sentimentality of the faculty. "Today's student learns more easily from a television screen than from a book," he insists. Mr. Cornberg's advice to campus planners is explicit: "My advice is: plan no more buildings for library use. The library space is a concession to the past. Don't invest in bricks and mortar!"

WHEN IS TOMORROW?

What stands between the library of today and this smoothly efficient, precision-machined tomorrow?

Plenty.

Before the library of the future can become a reality—if, indeed, we want it to—a number of towering intellectual, technological, and economic barriers must be hurdled. This is not the place to rehearse these all in detail. But a look at only a few of them impresses one with their complexity.

As human knowledge expands, becomes ever more splintered into subspecialty and sub-sub-specialty, and the relationships between specialties become more important, it becomes necessary to improve profoundly our system for the classification of knowledge. The utility of any system of information retrieval, whether manual or automatic, depends most heavily on how finely the data in the memory bank is classified and cross referenced. Before large masses of vital knowledge are committed to a machine mind, it is absolutely essential that systems of classification be so highly developed that nothing of significance will be lost. Yet today we do not know enough about logic, semantics, psychology, and the structure of knowledge to code all existing information so that we can safely pull it out of a storage unit.

The problem of classification is essentially an intellectual problem. It has nothing to do with nuts and bolts. But it is growing ever more difficult as the volume of information expands. As one researcher has pointed out, "The difficulty of assigning something to the *right* pigeonhole is greater, the greater the number of pigeonholes. It is thinkable that for a sufficiently large and detailed subject list, a point of considerable doubt may be reached as to whether two people (for example, cataloger and user or reference librarian) would agree on a classification assignment often enough to permit the system to work at all. This problem may be one of the most important consequences of information growth."

Today scholars at Harvard, University of Minnesota, University of Iowa, Western Reserve University, and elsewhere are digging into the terminological or classification problems of information retrieval. But until human knowledge, seen as an organic system, is better understood, and a reliable and

sufficiently sophisticated system of classification is agreed upon, we are not going to be ready to use machinery, simply because, as one expert puts it, "we don't dare run the risk of losing information."

Machines have been developed that can index and classify material automatically, by recognizing certain key words in the material and matching them against a list of categories. Studies indicate, in fact, that these machines can index and catalog faster and more accurately than human catalogers. But how well they can do this depends entirely upon the refinement of the category lists fed into them and the sophistication of their programs— both dependent upon the human brain, and both not yet developed to anywhere near the point necessary for feeding whole libraries into little black boxes.

Moreover, there are certain kinds of retrieval that a human reference librarian can perform that no known machine can. This is retrieval based not on objective factors, but on associative recall, a wholly subjective process. As one information retrieval specialist has explained it: "The machine may be able to get me a copy of Shannon and Weaver on 'The Mathematical Theory of Communication' if I ask for it and describe it correctly. But it cannot, if I misidentify it. Yet I can ask a librarian for a copy of that red book by Shannon on information theory, and somehow, through a process of association she will remember

that it is, in fact, an orange book, and that it is the one that has been circulated a lot recently to faculty members in the math department, and that its title is not what I said. She can find it for me despite my misinforming her." A good deal more work must be done on human psychology and perception before the machine can match this capability. "For a long time," says this expert, "the first step in information retrieval will be a conversation between a user and a librarian."

Another and related problem is the difficulty of reducing data to machine language. This is not a problem in those systems which, like WALNUT, simply reduce the physical size of the document. But for those methods that depend on reducing the *content* of books through abstraction, this problem is critical. These systems may begin with a scanning device that "reads" the data submitted for inclusion in the system and converts it into machine readable form. Automatic reading is done through "pattern recognition"— that is, the machine is constructed so that different patterns of sight or sound, say, a letter of the alphabet printed on a white background or spoken against a backdrop of silence, trigger certain responses in the machine. Optical and magnetic scanners that do this have received much publicity in the popular press. Yet the fact is that no machine yet exists that can "read" or "recognize" more than a single typeface.

Today every library of consequence

contains materials printed in as many as 1,000 different typefaces, plus a great volume of data in foreign languages and in alien scripts. Donald Black of U.C.L.A. cautions: "The large academic library will have mountains of retrospective material that cannot be put into machine readable form in the foreseeable future. You can't even get catalogers nowadays who can read Sanskrit. Where are you going to get a keypunch operator who can? Or a machine?"

In addition to such intellectual and technological obstacles to the achievement of true automatic information retrieval, there are many social and economic difficulties. It is important to remember that information retrieval must do better what is done by nonautomatic means—not merely equal it — before it stands a chance of being adopted. Small systems are already being used by certain corporations and by government agencies. But for most purposes, campus libraries have no need for the speed of retrieval that automatic systems would make possible. And they do not have the money to pay the freight. Don R. Swanson, a trim, imaginative, but hardheaded researcher, manager of the Synthetic Intelligence Department, Thompson Ramo Woolridge Inc., is busy developing ways to accomplish automated information retrieval, and he serves on a committee exploring its possible application to the Library of Congress. But Mr. Swanson cautions against the idea that automatic data recovery is around the corner.

"A complete set of Reader's Guide in conventional form," he points out, "provides 30-second access to 1-1½ billion bits of information stored in less than half a cubic yard of space, and a Boeing 707 filled with books and mail is so fantastically more efficient than the same amount of information transmitted electronically that it would seem a long time before electronic transmission can compete."

The idea that the book is already obsolete fills Mr. Swanson with contempt. "Right now the economics of automation are such that no present equipment economically threatens the book. This might change 10 years from now, but it'll be a long time before the book goes. What's more, any system of carrels hooked up to the Library of Congress or to regional depositories for remote TV reading of books or textual material is visionary and impractical on a national scale in anything like the next decade or so. People who talk this way are glossing over 20 years of engineering and several billion dollars of expense. Can it be done? Sure. Technically. But you've got a lot of things other than technical problems to consider!"

One of these, of course, is economics. First there is the cost of designing the system—the so-called "software" cost. There is no way now to estimate the cost of designing the kind of vast and comprehensive systems envisaged by those who advocate fully automatic retrieval systems encompassing the data in whole libraries. One rule of thumb suggested by Dr. Robert M. Hayes, president of Advanced Information Systems Co., is that this part of the job often winds up costing roughly the same amount as the hardware—the machines themselves. These, obviously, represent the second major element of cost and may range into the multimillions of dollars when computers, printers, transmission facilities, and all related apparatus are taken into consideration. Next, there is what Dr. Hayes calls "the really significant cost—that of getting the material into a form that the machine can handle." This means the translation of text into machine language and its subsequent preparation in the form of punch cards or tapes. Finally, there are the operating costs. Too little is known about any of these factors to make any real judgments. But all commentators agree the magnitudes involved are fantastically large for the complete data recovery systems under discussion.

The application of computers and punch card systems to clerical processing functions may be accomplished for far less expenditure and far more easily than the automation of information retrieval in the popular sense. For this reason, say experts like Dr. Hayes, the machine will find its place in the library. But not for information retrieval purposes for a long time to come. How long that time may be, he suggests, is a function of how badly automation is needed. For an institution like the National Library of Med-

icine, whose data must be available on demand and as quickly as humanly possible, the investment in I. R. can more easily be justified than an equivalent investment for a library that serves no essential research purpose or faces no intense urgency of demand.

Frank B. Rogers, director of the National Library of Medicine, and one of the most knowledgeable experts in the country on the application of machine techniques to the library, refuses to speculate on how long it will be before automatic information retrieval becomes a fact for most libraries. "If so little exists now, how can we extrapolate from it to make a prediction?" he asks. "All I know is that it is now possible to put the entire contents of the Library of Congress into a little black box. But it would take another black box 10 times the size of the Library of Congress just to provide the juice to run it!"

BUILDINGS OF THE FUTURE

Before it committed itself to plans for a library at Edwardsville, Illinois, Southern Illinois University dispatched consultant Donald G. Moore to survey the technological advances that might affect its decision. Mr. Moore interviewed 43 experts employed by companies like IBM, Lockheed, the Martin Company, Information Handling Services, System Development Corporation, Thompson Ramo Woolridge, Teleprompter Corporation, and R.C.A., as well as at the Stanford Research Institute, and the University of California Radiation Laboratory. His preliminary report presents a striking and imaginative picture of the possibilities of the future. But his findings clashed directly with the views of Mr. Cornberg. The report declared: "There was nothing found that would conflict with the conclusion that the Edwardsville campus should have a book-containing library."

This conclusion is shared by hundreds of other librarians, architects, scientists, and technical experts. The present large-scale assault on the problems of information retrieval and storage, Mr. Moore reported, "is certain to have an impact on modern library facilities," within 10 years. But not so deep an impact as to make the library of books obsolete.

Today the library profession is watching the technological revolution with hawk-like concentration. "We know," says Ralph Ellsworth, "that the era of the 'handcraft' library is at an end." But this does not wash away the pressing need for new libraries *now*, the miracles of technology notwithstanding.

Today hundreds of colleges and universities go ahead with plans for new and better libraries than ever before. At the same time, they are keeping an eye cocked on the future, preparing for it as best they can. Hollow floors and ceilings going into new buildings are concealing miles of electrical conduit and ventilation ducting so that computers, punch card machines, TV screens, or other devices can be plugged in at any point. At U.C.L.A., alert to the possibilities, a pneumatic tube planned for a new building was increased in diameter so that it might carry IBM cards without the need for them to be folded.

At the National Library of Medicine, which has had more experience with the machine age than any other library in the country, preparations are being made for bringing in a computer so that it may improve and speed up the work now done by punch card equipment in the compilation of *Index Medicus*. The changeover has meant the installation of a false floor in the computer area to contain the wiring required and to serve as a plenum to dissipate the heat generated by the machine. Such floors now come in standard modular sections so that any section can be pulled out at will. A special 50-ton air conditioner is being readied, and another set aside for emergency service. Space is being allotted for the computer, for related machines, for parts and test equipment. A special fireproof vault is being built to store the precious magnetic tapes—the computer memory—when they are not in use.

The lack of extensive experience to date makes it impossible to predict accurately all the adjustments that must be made in the design of modern library buildings if they are to take full advantage of the coming age of automation. But the uncertainty that accompanies an age of rapid social and technological change proves the essential rightness of the modular revolution. For today, more than ever before, library buildings must avoid becoming frozen forms. They must be easily and swiftly convertible from one use to another. In the words of Ralph Ellsworth: "All we really know is that we should provide a good deal of uncommitted floor space that can accommodate rooms of varying size, each well-lighted, properly ventilated, with access to wiring ducts from which electrically powered machines can draw their power, with good soundproofing qualities. Such a building can be set up to meet the needs of the college at the present time and for the known future. This is about as far as our existing knowledge will permit us to go.... Our buildings should be capable of major expansion or of conversion to other uses."

The avalanche of technological discoveries, the accelerating pace of change may, as has been suggested, transform the library, eliminate the book, and provide still-unthought-of methods for collecting, storing, recovering, and communicating information. But for the foreseeable future the campus library, with all its primitive faults, will remain a vital part of our intellectual landscape. We need the know-how, money, and courage to make it just as good as is humanly possible.

DORMITORIES

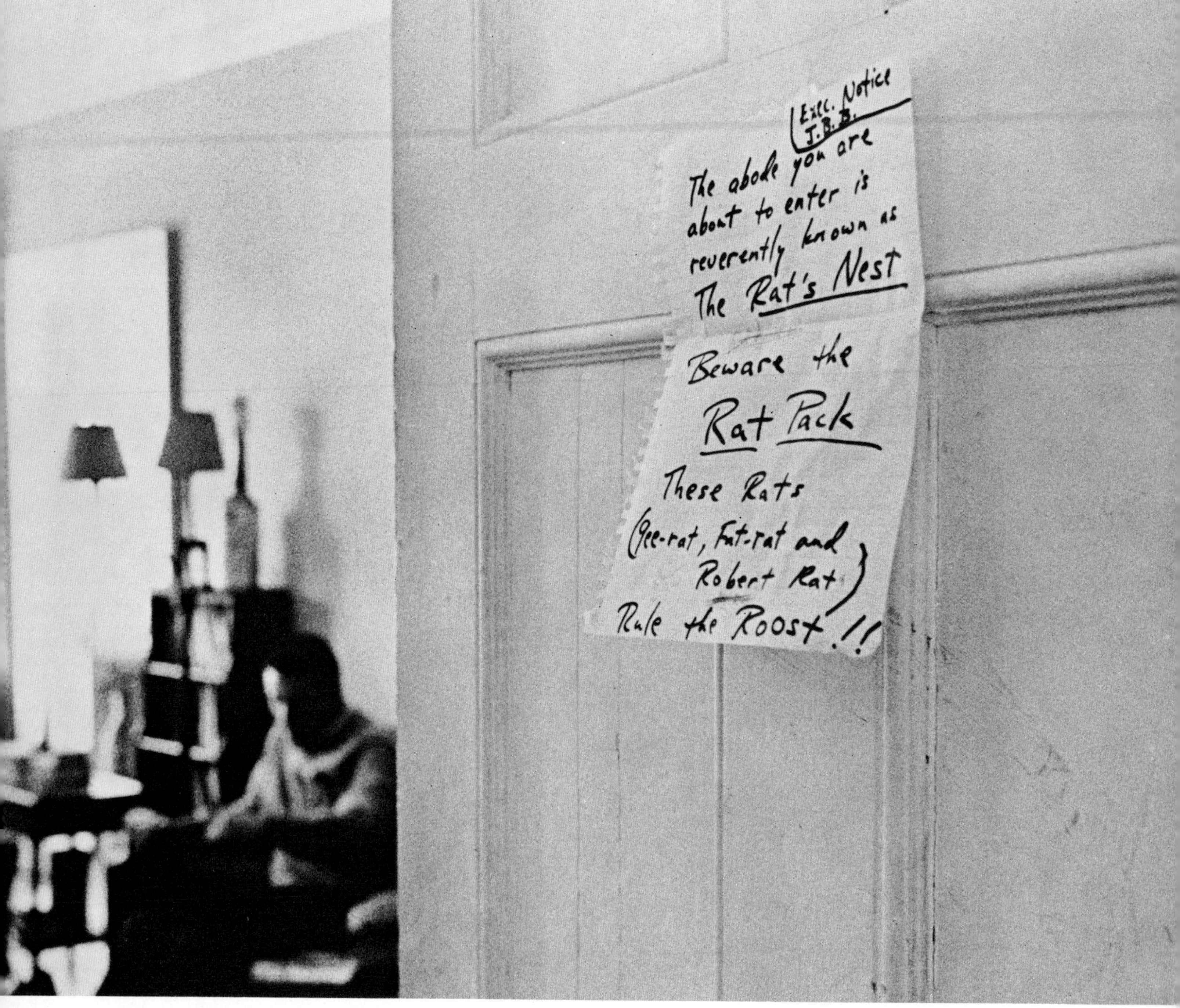
Exec. Notice
J.B.B.
The abode you are
about to enter is
reverently known as
The Rat's Nest
Beware the
Rat Pack
These Rats
(Gee-rat, Fat-rat and
Robert Rat)
Rule the ROOST!!

DORMITORIES
by
Margaret Farmer

Stephen Leacock once suggested that colleges should first provide a smoking room and a dormitory, and then, if any money were left over, hire a professor. None have followed his advice, but most of them grant that it was not wholly facetious. Educators from John Dewey on have expounded the symbiotic relationship between living and learning, and housing officers have for years paid tribute to the contribution good housing can make to education.

Yet, as Christopher Jencks and David Reisman point out in *The American College,* "At an average cost of roughly $4,000 per student, the typical student residence joins two students, two beds, two bureaus, two desks, two straight chairs, and 200 square feet of floor in an effort to produce enlightenment."[1] They might have added that the room they describe is one of hundreds of identical cells strung along endless corridors which reverberate with the rhythm of footsteps, the ringing of telephones, and the rush of water from the modern plumbing. The focal point of the cell block is the gang toilet where the floor residents meet for a daily lesson in togetherness. Finishes and furnishings, in and out of student rooms, are so pointedly durable they virtually dare the students to damage them.

The vast formal lobby downstairs is decorated to the last potted palm in a style that would do credit to any third-rate hotel. The student rarely uses it except for a brief uneasy chat with his visiting parents before he hustles them out of the dormitory and over to the nearest campus hangout for a cup of coffee and some relaxed conversation. He does use the basement recreation room because the coke machine and cigarette dispenser are there. Also, the ping-pong tables are big enough to spread books and papers on, and his desk is not.

There are no books in the dormitory outside the student's room, and since his bookshelf was designed to hold six standard-sized texts and no more, there are not many even there. There are no paintings except the portrait of the president which graces the lobby—unless, of course, the student has accepted the dare to damage the walls and has tacked up a print or two in his own room. There is, above all, as an observer of the college scene noted more than 30 years ago, "no place where he can sit down in comfort with a book and pipe and possess his soul in quietude, no place where he can entertain his chosen friends, where in a score of ways he can express and develop his taste and personality, his individuality."[2]

If this graceless shelter reflects some confusion about what good housing

[1] Christopher Jencks and David Reisman, "Patterns of Residential Education: A Case Study of Harvard," in *The American College,* ed. Nevitt Sanford (New York: John Wiley and Sons, Inc., 1962), p. 732.

[2] William McDougall, "Functions of the Endowed Universities of America," in *Higher Education Faces the Future,* ed. Paul A. Schilpp (New York: Liveright Publishing Corp., 1930), pp. 242-243.

is, it also raises some questions about what housing could and should contribute to education. A few years ago, the housing director at a large university summarized the educational objectives of the residence hall program as the teaching of "leadership, cooperation, good citizenship, and social competence." So far, so good. But many college administrators are wondering whether housing might not promote learning as well as leadership, academic competence as well as social competence—and if so, by what kind of physical arrangement and design.

This revival of interest in housing as an instrument of learning can be traced to factors as many and diverse as the colleges themselves, but high on the list is the sheer pressure of numbers. For while every college facility from the library to the power plant will be jarred by the impact of the seven million students who are expected to arrive on campus by 1970, housing will bear the brunt of the pressure: in a pinch, more students can be jammed into a classroom, but the limit to the number of students who can be shoe-horned into a bedroom built for two is quickly reached.

Just to keep pace with their doubling enrollments, American colleges, which in 1960 housed one million students, will have to build housing for at least another million by 1970, and there is every indication that the need for new housing is increasing even faster than enrollments. Some of the students housed in 1960 were the third

man in a two-man room, or the occupants of a hastily improvised dormitory in what was once a recreation room. Many of them lived in buildings so run down that they would have to be omitted from any inventory of acceptable housing. (The barracks and quonset huts so many colleges threw up after World War II to cope with the sudden influx of married G.I.'s are the most obvious example, but almost every campus also has at least one relic of an earlier era, which is regularly scheduled for retirement and just as regularly filled with the overflow from newer dormitories.)

Any realistic estimate of the housing job to be done in the sixties must take into account the new units needed to clean up this backlog of unsatisfactory housing, as well as the units needed to house expanding enrollments. It must also take into account the probability that colleges will attempt to provide housing for more of their students than they have in the past—perhaps as much as 40 per cent of the additional enrollment.

In part, the anticipated increase in the percentage of students housed on campus reflects the growing conviction that the residential community can be a vital adjunct to the academic community. "This would seem a lot more like college," *The New York Times* quotes a Columbia University student, "if my professors didn't always disappear into the subway right after class." It would seem even more like college if the students didn't do

likewise—and since it makes little difference whether the point of dispersal is a subway or a parking lot, the 9-to-5 syndrome is no longer peculiar to the urban college. Many not-so-urban institutions are becoming commuter colleges in spite of themselves as more and more of their students and faculty members range farther and farther from the campus in search of a place to live. By expanding their housing programs, these schools, like their city cousins, hope to arrest the disintegration of the academic community that occurs when large chunks of its population vanish at the stroke of five o'clock.

For the most part, though, colleges are housing more of their students because they must. As enrollments swell, private housing within reasonable commuting distance of the campus simply cannot absorb the overflow from bulging dormitories. Married students and faculty members, left to fend for themselves, pore over the meager offerings of a boom market: "Bedroom, living room, kitchen. Furnished. No children. Utilities separate. Rent $175-225." Single undergraduates find themselves in over-priced, under-furnished rooms 40 minutes away from class.

Faced with a choice between sitting by while students and instructors combine their daily pursuit of knowledge with a nightly pursuit of cockroaches, or building enough housing to bring supply and demand into better balance, most schools prefer to build.

The one factor that threatens to brake the trend toward the colleges' assuming more of the housing burden is cost, which is following an upward trend of its own. Between 1955 and 1960, housing construction costs averaged about $4,400 per assignable space. But the Office of Education is already basing its cost projections to 1970 on an average of $4,700 per student, and most observers believe that steadily rising construction costs and steadily rising institutional standards make $5,000 a more realistic figure.

When it comes to predicting total expenditures for residential facilities in the next 10 years, the soothsayers' crystal balls cloud over. Largely because it is anybody's guess how close the colleges will come to meeting their housing needs, it is also anybody's guess how much money they will spend. The experts, whose estimates range from $2.5 billion to $6 billion and up, agree only that the amount will be staggering.

DOUBLE RETURN ON THE DORMITORY DOLLAR.

Since statistics never solved a housing shortage, most college administrators are less interested in the numbers, however impressive, than in the problems they delineate. Having long since bowed to the inevitability of providing more housing, they want to know how they can realize a fair return on the hefty investment required. Having concluded that while housing is seldom profitable, it can and should

be educationally productive, they want to know what kind of student living arrangement can be expected to yield educational dividends.

The earliest American colleges tried to answer the question by modeling themselves after the residential colleges then flourishing at Oxford and Cambridge. But the English variety of residential education never really took root in the New World. In the next great wave of college building, the proliferating state universities and land grant colleges took their cue instead from the continental universities: what the student learned was the college's affair; where and how he lived was not.

This *laissez faire* attitude toward student life persisted until the turn of the century, when the inevitable swing of the pendulum began. College campuses sprouted a bumper crop of new facilities—from student unions to infirmaries to dormitories—that reflected the educator's growing recognition of the student's physical and social well-being as a prerequisite to his academic progress.

In the rush to minister to the whole student, though, the colleges often forgot that he was, after all, a student. The gap between what the student learned and where and how he lived was not narrowed perceptibly when the dormitory began to supplant the boarding house, and the student union began to challenge the pre-eminence of the fraternity house as the central symbol of the collegiate fun culture. Students

continued to shuttle back and forth between the uneasily coexistent worlds of their peers and their professors.

For more than 50 years, educators have tried to weave together the stubbornly parallel strands of student life. Today, their redoubled efforts are bringing the American college full circle. For the point at which the strands converge is increasingly apt to be a residential program that harks back to the system the colonial colleges imported 300 years ago.

Thus, when George F. Baughman, President of the new New College in Sarasota, Florida, speaks of "building a great school by using the old ideas with new vitality," it is more than a pretty speech. The embryonic institution he heads will borrow not only its name but its basic approach to residential education from Oxford's 500-year-old New College. Most administrators are more wary of transplanting the residential college intact, but since they agree with the principle Baughman propounds, many have found it practical to graft selected cuttings from the English stock onto their own residential systems. The resulting housing programs are as varied as the colleges themselves. Yet the hybrids retain an essential similarity. All try to build a residential community that narrows the gap between teacher and student, classroom and living room. And all try to reap a richer yield from the huge investment in housing by creating a living climate that is also hospitable to learning.

EDUCATION IN RESIDENCE: THE YANKEE PROTOTYPES

Harvard's houses and Yale's colleges, as the oldest Oxbridge offshoots on this side of the Atlantic, are a logical point of reference for tracing the evolution of the domestic variety of residential education. Harvard and Yale were among the colonial schools that unsuccessfully aped the English system, but by the time they again looked to Oxbridge—and to their own past—for a model, that youthful fling was only a memory. Having joined the majority of American colleges in adopting a quasi-continental approach to higher education, neither school wished to be remade in the Oxbridge image. Like most colleges today, they chose to borrow only those aspects of "the collegiate way of life" that might complement and enrich their own established style of campus life.

Unlike most of their contemporary colleagues, however, Harvard and Yale did their borrowing some time ago. Each has operated a housing program based on the principle of education-in-residence for more than 30 years. And each has recently presented concrete evidence — Harvard through three-year-old Quincy House and the more recent additions to Leverett House, Yale through the new Stiles and Morse Colleges—that it considers the venture into residential education a success.

The experiment began in the late twenties when oil magnate Edward Harkness, a Yale alumnus, offered to house every upperclassman at Harvard and Yale in residential colleges on the Oxford-Cambridge model. Both schools welcomed the gift as a possible means of bridging the yawning chasm between the academic world of their faculties and the social whirl of their students. But while Harvard's President Lowell permitted himself a wistful vision of "gentlemen around the breakfast table," neither school's administrators were nostalgic or naive enough to hope that the new housing would magically create a community of scholars. Instead, they undertook their experiment with the modest goals of loosening the stranglehold of the social clubs on student life and restoring communication between students and teachers.

The facilities with which they set out toward these goals were not so modest. Calculated to compete with the often-splendid headquarters of the clubs, they typically included single rooms, frequently combined in suites, for 250 to 300 students; more lavish living quarters for the master and his family and a dozen or so other resident faculty members; a library of 10,000 to 15,000 volumes; common rooms for students and faculty; game and music rooms; offices and seminar spaces; guest suites; and a large dining hall where nonresident tutors and other faculty members associated with the house or college could join students for meals.

Although the new buildings are necessarily less munificent than their predecessors, they offer essentially the same facilities, which makes them luxurious indeed compared to the general run of college dormitories and raises the question of what they contribute to the student's education besides a high standard of living.

The most frequent criticism leveled at the house plan is that, in spite of the resident faculty, the library, and other outward trappings of a scholarly community, it does not really unite the students' academic and social life. Though tutorials and occasional discussion groups are conducted in the living units, instruction remains centered in the academic departments. The resident faculty is apt to be composed of unmarried graduate students and instructors rather than full-fledged professors. The nonresident professor's commitment to his house is often casual.

Such criticism is valid in part, although new factors in the house system equation tend to make it less so. The increased emphasis on independent study, for example, offers a natural opportunity to shift the focus of some areas of academic work from the classroom lecture to tutorials, seminars, and other types of instruction that are at home in the living room. And both Harvard and Yale have broadened the faculty circles from which they can recruit tutors and fellows by providing in their newer buildings family apartments as well as the traditional bachelor suites, making it possible for the not-so-junior scholar

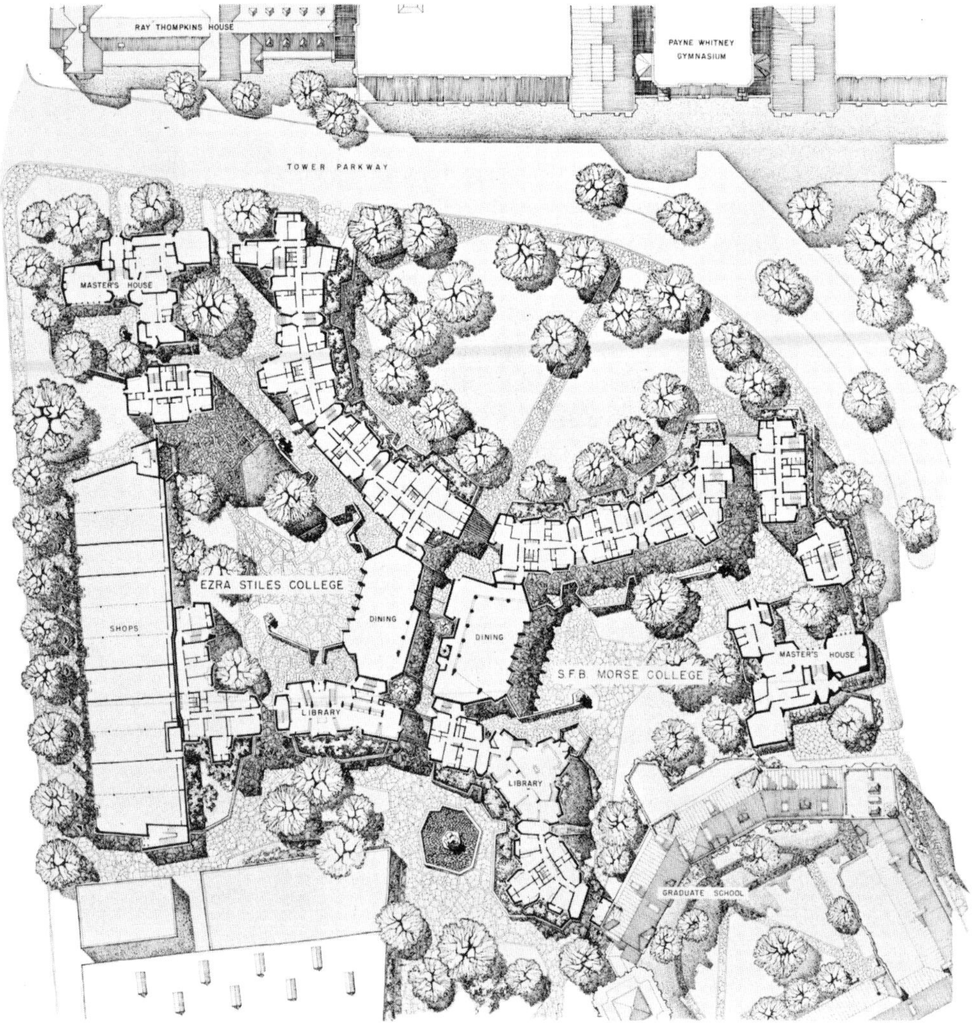
RAY THOMPKINS HOUSE
PAYNE WHITNEY
GYMNASIUM
TOWER PARKWAY
MASTER'S HOUSE
EZRA STILES COLLEGE
SHOPS
DINING
DINING
S.F.B. MORSE COLLEGE
MASTER'S HOUSE
LIBRARY
LIBRARY
GRADUATE SCHOOL
BROADWAY

The irregular exterior of Yale's Stiles and Morse Colleges gives their interior living spaces variety, individuality—and style.

to participate in the house community without tripping over undergraduates at every turn.

The most telling retort to the critics, however, is that neither Harvard nor Yale had at the outset any intention of making Mr. Harkness' residential colleges academic units. They hoped merely to make them living units that might provide an intellectual middle-ground between the club and the classroom. In this sense, the experiment has, on the whole, accomplished what it set out to do.

The effect such a residential community has on the total educational process resists precise measurement. But those who have lived with one for thirty-odd years are convinced that "students and faculty members, associating in these residential units, can do much to educate one another in ways that are not encouraged by the formal curriculum."[3] And since this belief lies at the heart of residential education, the Harvard-Yale experiment has become the point of departure for much of the more recent experimentation with new patterns of student housing.

In addition, many schools that find the contents unassimilable admire the new packages. The Stiles and Morse Colleges at Yale, for example, are distinguished by a ruggedly irregular exterior that leaves its stamp on the interior as well. Rooms ramble along corridors whose erratic twists and turns define, without physically separating, the vertical sections into which

[3] Jencks and Reisman, *op. cit.*, p. 732.

the four-story residence halls are divided. A few entry units contain only single rooms, but most combine single rooms with suites for two, three, or four men in floor groupings informal enough to offer each of the college's 250 residents a convenient outlet for his social instincts without forcing him to join a herd. The student's own room also respects his sense of individuality: it is probably trapezoidal rather than rectangular in shape, and even if it boasts four square corners, it is apt to have an oddly shaped window or some other feature that marks it as unique—and his. "Stiles is the next best thing

to a garret—*la vie bohème* with plumbing," an enthusiastic resident reports.

At Harvard's Quincy House, the raffish garret becomes a properly—and elegantly—Bostonian flat. Because the building sandwiches a living room floor between pairs of bedroom floors, each of its four-man suites is a self-contained duplex apartment with single rooms and bath one flight above or below a comfortable sitting room. Some of the arrangement's advantages are obvious: the book-bent student who finds his suite-mates in the midst of a vehement discussion need not choose between joining in and leaving the

apartment; he can also retreat to his own room to study undisturbed by the noise from the living room.

The duplex scheme has hidden assets as well. Since the bedrooms are accessible from the suite living rooms, corridors are omitted from the building's four bedroom floors and the space they would have consumed is put to more productive use. (Fire doors between the baths provide a second emergency exit and access for cleaning and maintenance.) Elevators need stop only on the two living room floors, making vertical circulation faster and more economical. And such potentially noisy areas as the corridors and living rooms are physically separated from the sleep-study areas where quiet is important.

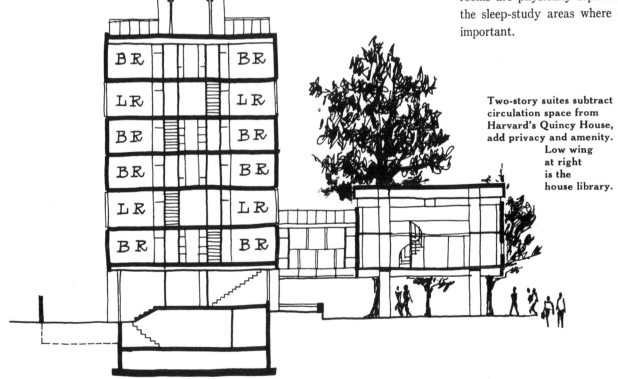

Two-story suites subtract circulation space from Harvard's Quincy House, add privacy and amenity. Low wing at right is the house library.

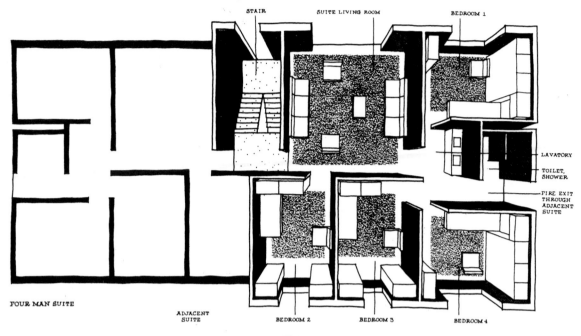

STAIR SUITE LIVING ROOM BEDROOM 1

LAVATORY
TOILET, SHOWER
FIRE EXIT THROUGH ADJACENT SUITE

FOUR MAN SUITE

ADJACENT SUITE

BEDROOM 2 BEDROOM 3 BEDROOM 4

Private rooms in four-man suites are the basic building block in the graduated social hierarchy of a new University of Pennsylvania house plan.

FOUR MAN SUITE

A TRADITION IN THE MAKING

Among the schools that have decided the Harvard-Yale approach to student housing offers values more durable than an opportunity for conspicuous consumption is the University of Pennsylvania, which recently announced a long-range proposal for reorganizing its undergraduate men's housing around a series of residential houses.

Penn's decision to adopt a house plan, and to revamp its existing residence halls to match the pace set by the new houses, is relevant here less because the University of Pennsylvania shares the aims that have led other colleges to consider one or another variety of residential education than be-

cause it also shares the dilemma that has forced so many of them to reject this particular variety as impractical.

It became apparent a few years ago that the familiar combination of projected enrollment increases, plus a dwindling supply of suitable off-campus housing, would soon add up to an unprecedented drain on the university's housing resources. Penn responded with an intensive study of how it could best meet the stepped-up demand for dormitory space, taking as axiomatic the proposition that the housing program should expand in a direction that would further the university's long-term goals. And since residential education is a logical goal for a school that will ultimately house upwards of 75 per cent of its under-

graduate men, the house plan proposal was the result. (The existing women's dormitories will also be organized into houses for the university's relatively small female enrollment.)

Although the proposed residential system is carefully tailored to the University of Pennsylvania, it was clearly cut from the Harvard and Yale pattern. Like the prototype house plans, Penn's will rely heavily on the ability of a faculty staff—the House Dean; a resident Junior Faculty member for every 30 students; and a Senior Faculty which is nonresident but has office, lounge, and seminar space within the house—to create the vigorously intellectual social climate that is the hallmark of the successful house plan. And like them it will support the staff by providing a physical environment that can, in itself, help reinforce the aims implicit in the concept of residential education.

The design of the houses is based on the assumption that a student residence can be judged by how well it meets two fundamental student needs: privacy and participation in a civilized community. The planners felt that only a room of his own, with a door he can shut—or even slam—will give the student any real sense of privacy. But they also felt that a haphazard collection of student rooms, single or not, is a community only in the loosest sense. So, taking the single room as the basic building block, they constructed a graduated hierarchy of social units.

The smallest social unit is a suite of four student rooms organized around a common living room. Suites are then paired and stacked four high so that 30 students, and the Junior Faculty member who serves as their counselor, share one stair and entry. Finally, eight 30-man subhouses are joined around an enclosed courtyard which gives access to the house dining hall, library, and other common facilities. Thus the total house population is around 250—small enough for each resident to know the others by name, but large enough to support the common facilities provided, including efficient food service. (The house community will also include 50 nonresident students who will be assigned to one of the Junior Faculty members for coun-

seling, given a place to store their books, coats, and tennis rackets, and otherwise encouraged to take advantage of the special programs and facilities the house offers.)

The University of Pennsylvania departs from the Harvard-Yale model in that it is not continuing an established tradition, but creating a new one in the course of doubling its housing capacity. Why, then, did it choose a residential program as costly in facilities and staff as the house plan?

"We wanted it," replies Howard Taubman, who, as director of the University Planning Office, was the moving spirit behind the housing study and the resulting proposal. "And we were willing to pay for it."

At an estimated $10,000 a student, the proposed houses will cost half again as much as the university's most recent and most comparable residence hall, but the difference in price is hard to pin down, in spite of undeniably expensive "extras" like the library and the living quarters and other spaces provided for the faculty. For while comparisons mean little unless purely housing costs are separated from costs that would ordinarily be charged to instruction, the very nature of a house plan defies such an orderly (and arbitrary) financial breakdown. Labeling its spaces "living" or "learning" may shed some light on the nature of the extra costs of the house, but the administration prefers to concentrate on the extra contributions it will make.

A HIGH-RISE HOUSE PLAN, CHICAGO STYLE

The University of Chicago, never fond of playing follow-the-leader, began experimenting with residential education almost 40 years before Harkness equipped Harvard and Yale with housing laboratories, and its results differ from theirs in form, if not in substance. The house plan that evolved from Chicago's early dormitories resembles its Eastern cousins in its emphasis on a faculty-led intellectual community, but it has remained on speaking terms with housing systems more conventional in organization and more modest in facilities. As a result, many schools that consider the Harvard-Yale version of residential education too radical or too costly see the approach exemplified by Chicago's Pierce Hall as merely a logical development of their own housing programs.

Pierce Hall, the first of two projected 10-story towers, has a total student population (around 320 men) within the range considered manageable as a house community, and it has the library, dining hall, and commons which are the characteristic appurtenances of a house. But the hall is not the house. Rather it contains four houses, each occupying two floors of the tower.

Since they share the building's common facilities, these 83-man units correspond roughly to the entries or subhouses of the orthodox house or, for that matter, to the wings, precincts, and floor groupings of the typical large

109

residence hall. However, great stress is placed on establishing their identity as houses in their own right, rather than mere physical subdivisions within the larger community. Each has its own name, its own faculty staff, its own assigned section of the dining hall, and even, since the skip-stop elevators stop at each house instead of each floor, its own entrance.

The houses themselves are built around two-story living rooms which puncture a service-circulation core that contains bathrooms, study and typing rooms, music rooms, and other shared facilities. As the house commons, this central living room is a natural focus for the social and intellectual life of the house as a whole. It is also a convenient gathering place for individual house members, who live in conventional two-man study-bedrooms instead of the suites and singles which have become almost synonymous with house plans. In the final analysis, though, Pierce Hall's living units are houses not because they are properly

labeled and equipped, but because they are led by a faculty member rather than a counselor-cum-housemother or an advisor-cum-proctor. The Resident Head for each house is assisted by a graduate student or senior who also lives in the house, and by eight nonresident Faculty Fellows who lunch there regularly and attend house meetings and programs.

(The strict separation of the units discourages the student's mingling informally with faculty members not directly associated with his house, but, as house plan critics have pointed out, there is no particular magic in juxtaposing students and teachers. For many students, a close association

with one faculty member may be more stimulating than a nod-across-the-dining-table relationship with several.)

Since Pierce Hall's faculty staff has no formal teaching responsibilities within the houses, its principal mission is to guide the students through the groves of academe, pointing out items of interest along the way. This inevitably means counseling of the personal as well as the academic variety, but it also means fostering the kind of atmosphere that enables Chicago's housing director to report flatly,

The University of Chicago's Pierce Hall features stacked two-story houses. Student rooms are ranged around a central house commons (right and on facing page). The dining hall and other communal areas are in the low pavilion.

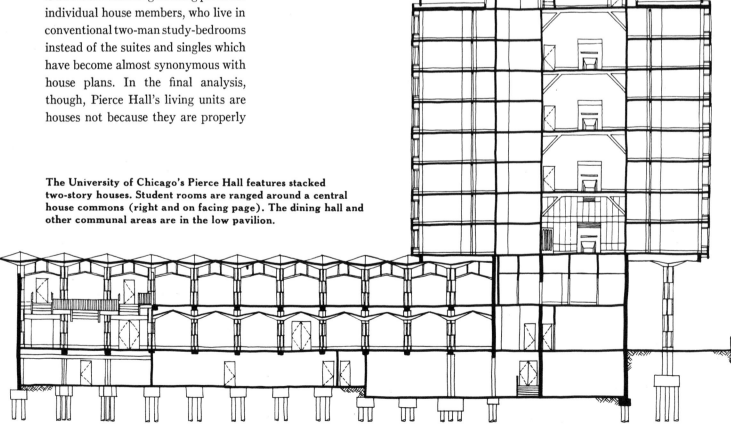

"Stressing intellectual activity in the residence halls is not a problem for us."

In many cases, the students themselves have taken the lead in organizing discussion groups, theater parties, how-to-study sessions for younger house members, and the like. This undoubtedly reflects Chicago's long tradition of personal independence, but it may also reflect the relative ease of communication within the small, tightly knit house groups.

If a house plan is to work at all, the community must be large enough to support such facilities as its own library and dining hall. Yet 300-odd students packed into double bedrooms and stacked 10 stories high can hardly be expected to experience the whole residence hall as a community, no matter what resources they are offered in the way of common facilities or faculty staff. By creating comprehensible neighborhoods within the larger community, the small houses with their individual commons do through formal organization what suites and sub-houses do less formally but often more expensively. Although Pierce Hall cost $6,740 per student, this figure includes a disproportionate share of the cost of the food service facilities, recreation rooms, and lounges in the adjoining 2-story unit. The per-bed price will drop to well within the average range for high-rise halls of similar size when the second of the proposed towers is built and the cost of these common areas spread among a larger student population.

HOUSING ON THE ELECTIVE SYSTEM

Stanford University's house plan, like Chicago's, is based on small living groups which are themselves houses rather than incidental subdivisions of a larger house community, and its program stresses personal rather than tutor-tutee relationships between house members and the faculty staff. Its principal departure from the traditional house plan format, though, is not in program or physical organization but in population. For Stanford's commitment to the principle of residential education is matched by its willingness to modify the practice to fit the needs of existing student groups.

Freshmen, for example, are usually quartered in conventional dormitories and promoted to a house only when they reach upperclass standing. At Stanford, the residence hall reserved for first-year students is actually a group of eight small houses which are not merely an introduction to the Stanford house plan, but its foundation.

By giving new students an opportunity to build close ties with the house faculty, the older students on the house staff—and each other—Stanford hopes to help them develop the intellectual maturity they need to participate in the broader academic community, and the social maturity they need to choose wisely among the housing electives open to upperclassmen.

Roughly one-third of the freshmen will elect to move on to one of the so-called "independent" houses Stan-

ford has set up in its existing upper-class dormitories, but this—or living off campus—is not their only alternative. The student may also join one of the fraternities, which at Stanford manage to feed and house a third of the upperclassmen who live on campus while fraternities elsewhere sink into a genteel decline. Or he may prefer one of the small eating clubs, whose members live in university housing but maintain their own cooperative dining halls and private clubrooms.

Although its hopes for expanding the house plan rest primarily on the growth of the independent houses, Stanford is taking pains to preserve the variety of housing patterns that now spices its campus life. So, unlike many schools, it encourages the traditional deviations from the new residential norm.

Williams College, for example, recently rocked the Greek-letter world by reclaiming from the fraternities its abdicated responsibility for providing their members with food, shelter, fun —and some educational resources that were conspicuously absent from the fraternity houses. Stanford, on the other hand, is leaving its fraternities intact as living groups as well as social groups, and building new houses for those that find it most difficult to feed their aging white elephants.

This fall, four fraternities moved into the first of the residential clusters in which the university is grouping its undergraduate houses. Four more fraternities will occupy a second cluster

which is now under construction, and similar clusters (a total of 10) will be added at the rate of one or two a year over the next 5 to 10 years to supplement, and eventually replace, the existing independent upperclass houses.

Each of the groups in the first fraternity village has its own separate house with two-man study-bedroom suites for 50 members in one wing; the dining room, a large living room that doubles as a chapter room, a library, and other social and study spaces in an adjoining wing. Future villages will follow the same basic pattern.

This cluster arrangement of separate but equal units makes it possible for the fraternities to preserve their autonomy without being burdened by the often exorbitant cost of maintaining autonomous houses. At the same time, it makes it possible for Stanford to draw the fraternity men into its program of residential education. The fraternity houses, unlike the independent houses, have no resident faculty, but all come under the tutelage of a faculty "master" whose residence is prominently placed at one end of the L-shaped cluster.

HOUSE PLAN PLUS...

The housing program Stephens College calls a "house plan" lives up to its name by creating an intellectually oriented living community in which students and teachers mingle freely

and informally. But since it brings the bulk of the students' classwork into the living room along with the teacher, it also exemplifies the more common approach to residential education which holds that learning can be brought into the residence hall, and more cordial relations established between student and faculty, without inviting the teacher to live with the students.

The 100 freshmen girls who live in West Hall, where the house plan was first introduced, take five core courses which are taught in the common rooms of the dormitory by five instructors, each of whom serves as advisor to 20 of the girls. Only one, who doubles as hall counselor, lives in the dormitory, but the others have offices in the hall so that they are in easy reach, and they have made a point of entertaining their advisees at home and otherwise encouraging informal contacts.

Charles Madden, who coordinated the work of the participating faculty during the first two years of the house plan, reports, "With all of us teaching the same students, we could try a lot of things we couldn't do with the ordinary talk-and-test lecture course." The faculty celebrated its independence from the college-wide 50-minute hour by developing an effective team teaching approach, and by experimenting freely with flexible class scheduling, a variety of teaching aids, and a program of independent study liberally laced with tutorials and seminars.

This free-wheeling academic program is so firmly rooted in the dormitory that Stephens makes a point of introducing West Hall residents to the rest of the college by requiring them to take five elective hours outside the hall. Yet the house plan moves virtually all the participants' class work into the house without making it necessary to move the classroom in as well.

Physically, West Hall is a conventional dormitory with conventional double rooms lined up on both sides of a utility island. Common facilities are minimal: a small lounge on each of the three upper floors of the building; a recreation room, counselor's apartment, seminar room, and faculty offices on the ground floor. Except for the faculty offices and seminar room, none can be labeled educational, but the house plan gets maximum educational mileage from all of them. The lounges and recreation room are used for classes, one lounge doubles as the main lobby, another lounge houses a small library, and so on.

CLASSROOMS IN THE LIVING ROOM

Though the Stephens experiment has drawn enthusiastic applause from both players and spectators, Stephens would be the first to admit that the plan requires a set of ground rules that many colleges simply could not follow. One, of course, is the need for a common core curriculum, which is now stymying Stephens' efforts to extend the house plan to more of its students. Another is the need for courses that are at home in the living room. (Stephens added a course in natural science to its second house plan dorm, found it was less successful than the original course offerings, and dropped it.) A teacher-student ratio as low as Stephens' 1 to 20 helps, too, as does the relatively small size of the residential group. And a key factor is probably a faculty that thinks of teaching as its principal mission, not a distraction from its scholarly research.

Nevertheless, a number of colleges for whom an in-residence academic program as extensive as Stephens' would be impractical are finding other ways to use housing for instructional purposes. Michigan State's President John A. Hannah, for example, includes in his long-range plans for the university a proposal for using the dormi-

tories for formal instruction, in order to facilitate communication between teachers and students and "improve the environment of learning." (The residence hall teaching program will also produce more tangible benefits, among them more efficient use of hall facilities and less travel time between classes.)

When President Hannah announced his platform in March, 1961, he called for "bold, imaginative action" to implement it. In the case of the residence hall plank, at least, he got it. Case Hall, which was then under construction, sprouted classrooms in the recreation areas, laboratories in what the blueprints labeled storage rooms, and faculty offices in the two bedroom wings. Six months later, it opened for business with 40 classes. Wilson Hall, the second unit in the complex, began operating in the fall of 1962, and Wonders Hall, which completes the group, will open for the 1963-64 school year.

The three halls, which will house a total of 3,300 students, each have two six-story living wings, one for men and one for women, with shared classroom, dining, and recreational facilities between. In Wilson and Wonders Halls, however, these shared facilities occupy a central unit which is connected to the living wings by low links containing the faculty offices, resident advisers' suites, study rooms, and other spaces that had to be fitted into Case's half-built dormitory areas.

Impromptu or not, Case Hall's teaching program went through the first year's trial performance with professional aplomb, largely by avoiding the pitfall of making the classrooms appendages to the dormitory rather than vital working parts. Unless classrooms are used entirely, or at least primarily, by residents, they add little to the dormitory but extra traffic and extra noise. But unless enough residents are taking the same courses, it is difficult to reserve the classrooms for their use.

Since more than 30 per cent of Case Hall's residents in the first year of operation were freshmen, and most of the rest were sophomores, this difficulty could be circumvented by concentrating on courses required under Michigan State's two-year program of general education, plus a few popular electives. The emphasis is still on general education courses, although by 1962-63 Case and Wilson combined had enough students to offer other courses as well.

Since most residents take two courses in the hall, classes are scheduled in two-class blocks with a half hour between blocks to give students time for the long trek to or from classes on the main campus. The half-hour free period also gives students and teachers an opportunity to adjourn to the coffee shop for continued class discussions, conversations — and coffee — and informal contacts are further encouraged by locating the professors' offices in the hall. A few girls in Case complained that student-teacher contacts were too informal: the presence of instructors and male advisees in the living wings prevented their exercising the feminine prerogative of wandering through the halls in robes and hair curlers. But the majority opinion on the new halls is the one headlined by the student newspaper after Case's first term of operation: "What's Case Like? A-OK Say Students."

MSU's arch-rival, the University of Michigan, has given residents of its East Quadrangle dormitory what it calls "a perfect roommate": a language laboratory whose sole purpose is to help them with homework. The experimental 10-booth language lab lets students tune in on language programs playing in a central laboratory several blocks away simply by dialing a number, much as they would place a direct long-distance call. In addition to making it possible for the language student to do his homework at home, the relatively inexpensive auxiliary lab offers a practical way of relieving the load on the central language laboratory.

But in spite of the clear advantages of bringing such substitute teachers into the residence halls, Michigan's branch language lab is one of the few instances in which it has actually been done. Even television, which is as ubiquitous a feature of the dormitory lounge as of the home living room, is rarely used for in-residence instruction, although a handful of schools are showing how its enormous teaching potential can be harnessed to the residence hall.

At Stephens, for example, house plan students meet in one of the common rooms to view a required telecourse called "Ideas and Living Today," and stay on for a post-broadcast seminar on the material presented. Closed-circuit television is used in

much the same way to augment faculty lectures in some other courses, and teachers occasionally combine their classes so that all can watch special network broadcasts.

Other schools are considering the use of televised survey courses like Stephens' teleclass in contemporary problems to supplement regular course offerings so that an engineering student, say, whose highly specialized training leaves little time for the humanities, could tune in on a course in literature before dinner, just as thousands of nonstudents tune in on "Sunrise Semester" before breakfast. And for colleges which are already experimenting with combinations of televised lectures and "live" discussion groups, the next step may well be to assign the lecture as homework and save class time—and teachers—for discussion.

Most colleges that plan to bring instructional television into the dormitories hope to do so without special facilities. Thus while the new Albany campus of the State University of New York will include a major television production center, programs developed there will enter the dorms via sets in each house living room. On the other hand, another New York university is betting that future developments in audio-visual equipment and instruction techniques will make it possible—and perhaps necessary—to bring the telecast to the student, not the residence hall. At Kimmel Hall, a new dormitory at Syracuse University, audio and video conduits have been run to each student room, so that students will be able to tune in on televised lectures, particularly in large section basic courses, or use the audio equipment for dialing selected tape recordings from a central collection of master recordings. However, the system is not operational; the conduit is there so that it can be made operational when the time is ripe.

That, in fact, is pretty much the story on mechanical teaching aids in dormitories. Just as the business man who insists on ultra-modern design for his company's offices goes home to a 20th century Tudor castle, the college official who points with pride to the up-to-the-minute equipment in a science building often balks at the notion of bringing instructional equipment into the dormitory. And this is hardly surprising. The concept of teaching dormitories is new, for all its antiquity, and the use of audio-visual aids for teaching, in or out of the dormitory, is still newer.

Nevertheless, the equipment is gradually gaining acceptance. Even the staunchest opponents of canned education put up no resistance at all to a recording of Dylan Thomas reading Dylan Thomas, or to a network television presentation of a Stravinsky-Balanchine ballet. A language lab merits only token resistance. The so-called "teaching machines" are still regarded in some circles as scientific horrors second only to subliminal advertising, but their opponents have plenty of time to change their minds. Programed instruction, like other products of educational technology, will prove itself in the classroom long before it reaches the dormitory.

But if the new-fangled teaching machines have not yet been accepted as standard dormitory equipment, the old-fashioned ones usually found in libraries have. Examples of libraries in residence halls could once be totted up on the fingers of one hand, beginning and ending with the 12,000-volume collections provided for residents of Harvard's houses and Yale's colleges. Today it would take several hands and a few toes as well. For while 12,000-volume libraries are costly, and therefore rare, many schools, especially large universities on large campuses, are setting up similar but smaller branch libraries in or near the residence halls to make reference material —often including record and art collections as well as books and periodicals—available close to home and to relieve overcrowding in the main library. The more usual pattern for a dormitory library, though, is to place a small collection of standard references, books commonly assigned for outside reading, and books and magazines for browsing in a lounge or study room.

Recently, colleges whose limited funds and facilities have discouraged their providing even browsing collections have found that the paperback revolution which brought Plato to the corner drugstore can also bring him to the dormitory. Case Hall's library, for example, includes a large collection of paperbacks which students may borrow for indefinite periods, with the proviso that they return them or pass them on when read. The students certainly borrow them: the paperback library is often stripped of all but 70 or so of its several hundred books. Similarly a spot check of Stephens' West Hall last year showed that of the 425 paperbacks in the house library, 220 were in circulation—2.2 per student—although the titles in the collection are not required reading, but were chosen as part of the faculty's effort to provide resources which could "create an atmosphere conducive to intellectual growth."

The Stephens faculty also selected paintings and other art works for the hall, as well as for their own offices, and exhibitions of the students' own productions are a regular event in house life. At Stanford, art objects for the house lounges are borrowed from the Stanford Museum or the library

and changed about every quarter, and a few houses are buying paintings and sculpture outright. Students at the University of Chicago can live for a term with Picassos, Braques, Miros, and other original paintings from a collection on loan to the University.

THE CASE FOR COMMODITY AND DELIGHT

The introduction of books, music, art, and sometimes even architecture to dormitories that used to provide bed and board and little more is symptomatic of the trend toward making the living environment conducive to learning. And the trend is not limited to schools which are setting up house plans or in-residence academic programs. Many colleges are opening the door of the residence hall to unstructured educational experiences simply by building and furnishing them in a way that respects the residents' needs as students and as human beings.

When Cornell University began planning a new women's dormitory which opened last year, it asked a group of coeds what they thought the designers should consider in drawing up the plans. According to a release from the University News Bureau, "The coeds appeared to agree on one thing. Even though the hall must be a large one, it should avoid the institutional look.... Long corridors, large common rooms, rows and rows of anything—all should be avoided whenever possible.

"The new dormitory should not be designed for a single large group of 500 women.... Rather it should be subdivided ... so that various small groups could do different things at the same time, and not always be subject to the pressures of the majority.

"They wanted a sense of intimacy in the interior of the building ... a situation where a woman could be herself, could follow her own interests without continuous interference or without interfering with other persons."

If the girls had tried, they could hardly have come up with a more accurate, or more scathing, description of life in the typical college dormitory. However, the building that emerges so clearly from their list of don'ts for dormitory design is no longer as typical as it once was. Almost all colleges, for varying reasons, and with varying degrees of success, are trying to purge their new residence halls of the institutional taint by breaking the amorphous mass of students up into small manageable groups where residents can find companionship without pressure to conform and privacy without isolation.

Often, the effort is a token one, which relies on organizational groupings created by drawing imaginary lines across the long corridors to produce a sense of we-ness among the dormitory denizens on either side of the border. More often, though, the organizational groupings are backed up, or even replaced, by physical groupings which are just as arbitrary. (When a group of housing directors was asked how 50 came to be considered the ideal number for a student group, it developed that 50 was also—coincidentally—about the maximum number a counselor could counsel or a maid clean up after.)

Until educators come up with a more precise rule of thumb than "the group should be small enough for everybody to know everybody else's name," the most successful subdivisions are probably the house-that-Jack-built type which combine several groups of various sizes and various degrees of formality. The University of Pennsylvania's proposed room within a suite within a floor within an entry within a house, for example, creates groups of 1, 4, 8, 30, and 250 students —which should be enough variety for anybody.

Three new vertical-entry residence halls at Washington University build similar groups within groups, relying almost wholly on physical rather than organizational subdivisions. Here, too, the basic unit is the suite, where six men in two double bedrooms and two singles share a living room and bath. However, there are four suites to a floor, with the suite living rooms all opening on a central stair hall so that residents can easily visit back and forth. (It has been suggested that the real common bond that welds the suite groups into a floor group is the common coffeepot in the small kitchenette they share.)

Communication between floor groups and building groups is encouraged by dividing common rooms among the three residence halls—a library in one, a lounge in another, and recreation rooms in the third. This arrangement makes it not only possible but necessary for students to mix with the residents of other buildings as well as with students who live on other floors of their own hall. It also prevented duplication of common facilities, which, combined with the fact that the stairs are the only circulation spaces in the buildings, helped keep the cost of the three halls down to around $4,000 per student.

Architect Gyo Obata, whose firm designed the buildings, comments that the suite plan makes the halls real centers for study and discussion because it assumes that students are adults. The same assumption can be made, however, by other types of dormitory plans. At their best, suites are probably the most desirable living accommodations to be found on American campuses. But suites *per se* are not the answer to the problems posed by mass housing. If they are not carefully designed as living units, and carefully related to one another, they may provide no more privacy and much less opportunity for a varied social and intellectual life than a well-thought-out grouping of double rooms.

In fact, while the debate rages on the relative merits of suites and singles, that much maligned compromise, the double room, is turning up in imaginative arrangements which go a long way toward replacing the anti-intellectual institutional atmosphere the Cornell coeds complained of with the sense of intimacy without interference they wanted. The dormitory they helped design, for example, is a concave-sided triangle that consolidates vertical circulation, mechanical services, and common rooms in a central core which divides each floor into three smaller wings—a device that is used fairly frequently to cut down the length of "rows and rows" of rooms and thus to form relatively small living groups.

Just as house plans and other efforts to approach more or less formal educational objectives tend to produce small living groups, core plans and other arrangements designed to create more desirable social groupings tend to be accompanied by a higher degree of physical amenity as well. If room groupings are smaller, the endless, bleak corridors can be shortened—or, in the case of the vertical house, eliminated altogether—with a corresponding reduction in corridor traffic and noise. If toilet facilities must be duplicated for each group, it may be little more expensive to replace gang toilets that require the services of two janitors and a plumber with semi-private baths that the students clean themselves. Small common rooms for each group may add up to more space than the usual formal lounges and recreation rooms, but they use the space more effectively for more purposes, making it possible to reduce the size and number of social and recreational facilities shared by the whole hall.

Moreover, many so-called luxuries are highly practical in their own right. Semi-private baths may not only reduce maintenance costs and permit more efficient use of space, but also make it easier to rent the dormitory to adults for meetings and conferences during school recesses. Air conditioning can increase the utilization of facilities by making year-round operation feasible as well as increase the productivity of students by making them comfortable. High quality construction and materials, though more expensive in the beginning, prove cheaper in the long run because the run is longer. Carpet, in student rooms as well as public areas, produces acoustical dividends and may be less costly than it seems at first glance. (The University of Wisconsin found that it cost only $5 more per student to substitute carpet for resilient tile in a 1,000-student residence hall, and studies show that a carpet's weekly vacuuming and semi-annual shampoo cost less than a tile floor's weekly mopping and monthly waxing.)

The most practical luxuries that can be introduced to the college residence hall, though, are those whose virtues are least measurable. At least one study has shown that students like to study in small rooms, preferably their own, alone, or with one or two other students. But no one has yet shown a correlation between the size of a stu-

dent's desk, the adequacy of his book-shelves, or the availability of a typing room or a library, and a student's grades. No scale has yet been devised for measuring the educational contribution made by a resident teacher or an in-residence teaching program. And schools like Lake Erie College, whose only competitive edge over the neighboring behemoth, Indiana University, is its small size and civilized, even sophisticated, physical setting, are hard-pressed to prove that a humane living climate is the magnet with which they attract the kind and number of students they want. Yet more and more colleges are providing their students with the surroundings of a gentleman and the tools of a scholar in the belief that these things do produce educational returns, tangible or not.

BALANCING THE HOUSING BUDGET

The biggest obstacle to higher dividends from college housing is the size of the initial investment. Residence halls that contribute more to the student's education than a base from which he goes forth to class are helping the American college to wring extra value from its housing dollars—and often to justify spending so many of them. But the dollars must first be found.

The gospel of residential education is not likely to win many converts among schools whose lack of housing is stunting their growth, whose cur-

tailed enrollment restricts their income, and whose limited income precludes their providing more housing. To colleges trapped in this vicious circle, any discussion of ways and means of building better student housing is merely frivolous: what they want to know is how they can afford to buy any housing at all. They already know they can't afford *not* to.

Yet many of the financial inventions and innovations being born of the have-not colleges' need for a practical way out of their dilemma can also help schools whose money problems are less acute. For few colleges are so financially robust that they can afford to reject categorically any economic nostrum capable of bringing their educational goals closer to realization. The healthy majority of colleges and universities which can rely on conventional sources of construction funds, (gifts, state appropriations and taxes, federal grants and loans, and, increasingly, bond issues) may have comparatively little trouble in finding the money to build new residence halls, but they too can improve their overall economic position with regard to housing.

For example, while revenue bonds have lately become by far the most popular way of financing new housing, project revenues alone are rarely enough to retire the bond issue and pay day-to-day operating costs as well. The housing finance picture is often clouded by mysterious accounting procedures which bury such oper-

ating expenses as salaries and building maintenance in nonhousing accounts; lump together income from rents and income from food services, which are usually more profitable (or less unprofitable); or assign funds unrelated to housing income to the reserve fund for housing debt. But the clouds do not obscure the main outline.

Most housing projects can balance their budgets only if revenues from room rentals (and board charges, if any) are supplemented by funds from other sources. This subsidy is usually paid out of net income from debt-free dormitories and food-service facilities or other auxiliary enterprises, but it may also be drawn from conference income, special student fees, general university funds, and so forth.

To some colleges, making up the discrepancy between housing income and outgo may entail little financial strain. To others, the prospect of doling out tightly budgeted funds to keep a residence hall on its feet may spell the difference between housing and no housing. But no school really boasts "extra" income. So both the have's and have-not's are exploring, factor by factor, the equation that has made self-liquidating (i.e. unsubsidized) housing almost as mythical as the unicorn.

Their first discovery is that the simple formula, income = outgo, is not so simple when it must balance housing construction and operating costs, which seem to have no ceiling, against receipts from room and board, which are limited by the size of the student's pocketbook. Although average room charges have gone up more than 60 per cent in the past 10 years, and almost all colleges plan additional rate increases, few educators believe that average rents can climb far enough and fast enough to match the pace set by soaring building and operating costs without pricing college housing beyond the reach of the typical student.

Because of the clash between reasonable rents and adequate revenues, which is complicated by a similar incompatibility between low initial cost and long-term operating economies, most colleges find it necessary to weigh the conflicting factors in the income-outgo equation according to their own scale of values. This often makes the formula insoluble, but it also makes it a more realistic, if less tidy, description of the practical relationships among the variables governing housing finance. Armed with its description of existing relationships, the college can change them enough to bring income and outgo into better balance and reduce the required subsidy—if necessary, by moving the relevant variables up or down on its value scale.

THE UNICORN IN THE PRAIRIE

For the college whose alternative to self-liquidating housing is inadequate housing or no housing at all, a better balance is not good enough. Income must equal outgo.

One of the more successful cam-

paigns against the housing subsidy has been waged by Parsons College, whose basic strategy is a classic pincer movement involving simultaneous advances on low income and high expenses. But while other colleges that use the same approach manage little more than a precarious equilibrium between housing income and expenditures, Parsons has achieved an imbalance so profitable that its dormitories pay for themselves in less than five years and then go on to pay for newer dormitories.

Parsons' opening gambit was the construction of dormitories for freshmen. These ranch style buildings, which required only light framing and contained, as the college understates it, "no built-in extras," were built for around $12 per square foot as against a national average of $17 or $18. Moreover, since the college has been able to hold maintenance and operating costs down to about $120 per bed per year, its total annual expenses for the freshman housing, including debt service, add up to only $300 per student.

Balanced against this is the gross income from per-student charges of $50 a month for bed and $70 for board. (The 1961-62 average at private liberal arts colleges was $27 for room and $48 for board.) And Parsons' real income from housing is even higher than the monthly rates imply. Its trimester plan means that housing and food service produce revenue during the entire year, and its practice of putting three freshmen in a space no

larger than the typical double room in effect increases by 50 per cent the income from every 200 square feet of bedroom. The net result is an annual profit of $237 per student, which makes the freshman dorms more than merely self-liquidating even without the substantial 50 per cent profit from food service.

Possibly because money-making is a suspect activity for a college, but probably because of the marked discrepancy between the $1,500 a year Parsons' freshmen pay for food and lodging and the standard of living they can buy with it, Parsons' highly profitable housing operation has been a prime target for criticism from its college colleagues. And the students who call the dormitories home complain bitterly about the three-to-a-room arrangement.

Yet whatever one thinks of the means, it is hard to quarrel with the end. Parsons was on the edge of bankruptcy eight years ago. Since then, it has increased its housing capacity tenfold, making room on campus for every entering student, without drawing on tuition, fees, or other income needed for similar rehabilitation of its academic program and facilities.

Moreover, a happier sequel to the story of the pay-as-you-go freshman dorms is now being written. With the aid of a small grant from EFL, Parsons recently pulled together a team of consultants headed by architect John Shaver and assigned them the task of demonstrating that self-liquidating housing and a humane living climate are not necessarily a contradiction in terms. At a cost of about $3,600 per student including furnishings, the college is now building for its upperclassmen 55-student houses composed of three separate units, each with private rooms for 15 students grouped around a common living room.

To encourage casual but purposeful meetings between the residents of the three tiny cottages that make up each house group, common facilities are split among the small units. One contains a large lounge-library-meeting room; another the housemother's apartment and 10 additional student rooms; the third a wood-paneled dining hall and small kitchen which ignore the doctrine that food-service facilities cannot be run profitably for fewer than 250 captive customers.

The low cost of the houses also covers some comforts of home that are more commonly found in a good resort hotel — air conditioning, wall-to-wall carpeting, indirect lighting, an individual lavatory in each student room, attractive finishes and furnishings, and even piped-in music via FM radios in each room.

How so much for so little? The savings stem from three factors. First, the cottages' compact hexagonal plan encloses maximum space with a minimum of wall area and virtually eliminates such circulation spaces as corridors and stairs. Second, the small size of the units made it possible to use a sim-

ple, inexpensive framing system of load-bearing brick and block walls. Third, although the units themselves are small, the project is not. Ground was broken for the first three clusters in October, 1962, and 28 three-cottage clusters housing over 1,500 students will be completed and occupied by June, 1965. The assurance of continuous work over a three-year period was an obvious inducement to the contractor's submitting a low bid, but the principal advantage of the project's scope was the opportunity it afforded for prefabrication. Since the cottages are identical, many building elements could be factory prefabricated and shipped to the site as needed.

A fourth factor helping to move the project from the red side of the college ledger into the black is the operating saving resulting from an unusually favorable financing arrangement. Parsons' president, Millard Roberts, is a strong proponent of conventional loans from private agencies as a source of funds for housing construction. If properly secured, he argues, such loans give the borrower maximum flexibility in using and repaying the borrowed money. Since short-term financing can be arranged, the college can realize substantial interest savings, and since loan payments can be met from any convenient resource, present and future revenues from the property are unencumbered.

Roberts' argument in favor of this approach to housing finance is supported by Parsons' current revolving

credit agreement with the House of Morgan, which reaches a new zenith in flexibility of financing. It makes no stipulation as to the disposition of money borrowed or the source of money repaid, so long as the outstanding debt at any time does not exceed a specified limit—$4.4 million in the first year. In practice, though, the open line of credit will be used primarily to finance the new upperclass houses, with construction funds drawn as necessary and repaid out of annual net income estimated at $49,000 per house. Moreover, since the construction loan for each $200,000 house, plus 5¼ per cent interest, can be repaid within about 4½ years, Parsons expects to construct all 28 units without incurring more than $1 million in new debt in any year.

The advantages of this financing arrangement are as obvious as the fact that the arrangement hinges on Parsons' proven ability to build and operate housing that will show a profit in a hurry—a rare talent and one that many colleges are not anxious to cultivate. But even those schools that cannot or will not charge rentals high enough to cover all their housing costs could charge more than they do now, and, if necessary, substitute direct aid to needy students for the present hidden but costly subsidy to every campus resident. They could also consider raising housing revenues by operating the residence halls all year round—if not as student housing, then as conference centers or even hotels.

And if they cannot finance their residence halls on the assumption that the buildings will turn a quick profit, they can probably reduce the required subsidy enough to benefit from private enterprise's dawning realization that college housing is a good investment.

ENTER THE ENTREPRENEUR

Parsons' example notwithstanding, direct borrowing from private lending agencies plays a surprisingly small role in financing college housing, and its role is expected to dwindle to almost nothing in the decade ahead, as private and public schools alike turn to revenue bonds as their primary source of construction funds for residential facilities.

This does not mean, however, that private capital's contribution to housing finance is also dwindling. On the contrary, financial lending institutions are a major and growing market for college revenue bonds, especially those issued by public colleges and universities. (Private schools have tended to lean heavily on HHFA financing.) And recently, private enterprise, which is far too enterprising to let so conspicuous a demand go unsupplied has entered the college housing scene through still another door. For if Parsons' approach to student residences—low costs, high income, and construction financing that ties up as little capital as possible for as short a time as possible—is alien to the typ-

ical college administrator, it is familiar enough to the typical businessman to have become the basis for the sudden mushrooming of privately built residence halls.

Since the privately owned dormitory is the direct descendant of the rooming house, and shares its ancient and not wholly honorable tradition, it can hardly be considered a newcomer to the campus, but its reappearance there is being greeted with mixed feelings. Many administrators feel that the very concept of off-campus, privately owned housing runs counter to the college's desire to assume proper responsibility for its students' out-of-class activities, and undermines its efforts to make residential education an attractive way of life as well as an intriguing theory. Others are more concerned because the private residence hall, which must show a profit, is usually more costly to the student than comparable college-owned housing— and too often comparable only to the least attractive specimens tucked away among the college's housing facilities.

But if the colleges have good reasons for looking this particular gift horse in the mouth, many have even more compelling reasons for accepting the help of private enterprise in wrestling with what seems to be a perpetual housing crisis. The University of Wisconsin, for example, has lived in peaceful coexistence with off-campus residence halls since three private dorms were built in the twenties. A sixth was

completed in the fall of 1962, and Wisconsin would welcome more. The university itself cannot get new residence halls built fast enough to keep up with increasing enrollments; it is required by the state constitution to give preference to Wisconsin residents, which leaves out-of-state students dependent on the uncertain local housing supply; and it feels that the builders are providing suitable facilities.

Wisconsin's only quarrel with the private residence halls is the complaint echoed on every campus where such facilities have become an unofficial adjunct to the institution's housing program: they cost too much. As a rule, privately owned dormitories charge the student anywhere from 50 to 100 per cent more than the university's going rate, and those in Madison are no exception.

Without the private dormitories, though, many of the students who spill over from university housing—particularly the out-of-state students—would have no place to go except another school. And since the price of a room is only part of the price of a diploma, Wisconsin views the high cost of private housing philosophically. "We have kids from New York," says housing director Newell Smith, "who pay $1,200 or $1,500 a year to live in one of the Student-Hiltons and think they're getting a bargain. Good schools back East charge easily that much for housing—and twice our tuition on top of it." Other schools that share Wisconsin's inability to build new residence

126

halls as fast as new students arrive to fill them, advance a similar argument for encouraging the construction of private residence halls in spite of the premium students pay for them. "We always have some students who can afford to pay more for housing than we can afford to charge for it," the refrain runs. "Offer them something worth the extra money, and they'll take it. And we'll have that much more room in our residence halls for students who really need an inexpensive place to live."

Privately built dormitories come in models to suit every taste and budget, but the original model, and still the most popular, is the dormitory owned and operated by a builder who has eyed the captive market for student housing and, on his own initiative, put up a building that conforms to the student's needs as he sees them, and to the college's regulations. Some colleges cooperate in the venture by approving—and occasionally providing—supervisory personnel, but on the whole, colleges shun direct involvement with the operation of privately owned residence halls, preferring to control conditions in such properties from afar, through their power to place them off-limits to prospective tenants.

Newer versions of the private dormitory necessarily involve the college in the venture because they shift the emphasis from private ownership to private financing. Under many of the latest schemes, in fact, the college becomes a client, who buys housing in a complete physical-financial package, and pays for it in easy installments.

One such scheme is being marketed by C.I.T. Financial Corporation, whose recently formed subsidiary, C.I.T. Educational Buildings, Inc., offers the college customer ready-made residence halls which are essentially variations on the garden-variety garden apartment building. The apartments are replaced by suites of four small double bedrooms grouped around a common living room and bath, but the basic structure of the typical two-story apartment house is retained except for minor variations in layout and facade treatment. (Of the first two projects built under the Campus Homes Program, one replaces interior corridors with exterior balconies, groups the units in an open U rather than a closed U, and uses brick and rustic wood siding instead of brick and shingles.)

The financial component of this package is more alluring than the architecture. Under a lease-back plan, the units are built on the college's land and rented to the college at between $225 and $250 per student per year for a maximum of 12 years. When the lease expires, the buildings—then fully amortized—become the property of the institution.

In this way the college gets needed residence halls in operation quickly, with no initial outlay, and pays for them out of income, without incurring a long-term debt. In addition, at the rates needed to amortize them in only 12 years, the buildings, then college property, should produce a tidy net profit.

However, the package also includes disadvantages that should be carefully weighed. One is that the low cost of the units depends on the use of standard frame buildings. The buildings are adaptable within limits, but the limits may be too narrow for some nonstandard conditions. Since frame construction is not intended to take the hard knocks a dormitory is subjected to, the structure may succumb to ills requiring costly maintenance and repair work. It may also conflict with local code requirements: one of C.I.T.'s first customers bowed out because the applicable building code demanded fire-resistant construction for all multiple dwellings.

Another potential trouble spot is that the lease payments do not cover the annual cost of maintaining, operating, or staffing the buildings—items that typically average close to $200 per student, and seldom run much less than $120. At the most conservative estimate, then, annual outlays for lease payments and operating expenses on the proposed residences would add up to some $350 per student. So unless the college customer already charges above-average rates, operates its residence halls on a year-round basis, or is willing to subsidize the difference, the standard complaint against privately financed housing stands under the lease-back agreement—and since the college will collect the rents, any necessary increase will not be attributed to the private businessman's inalienable right to a profit.

Other building-investment firms are promoting similar packages with similar advantages and disadvantages. One of the first to enter the field was O'Meara-Chandler, a Houston-based outfit whose housing package includes a somewhat wider range of physical facilities in a choice of three financial wrappings, thus giving the college more latitude in selecting the assets it considers most important and the liabilities it can live with most comfortably.

The principal asset the package offers is that the low cost of the dormitory units stems from the use of a standardized building technique rather than a standardized building. With the lift-slab system employed, a permanent, fire-resistant structural shell (concrete slabs and steel columns) can be erected quickly and inexpensively, and finished off by simply adding outside walls and inside partitions. The system also gives a high degree of flexibility in arranging interior spaces, although the exterior variations are limited to variations in wall materials and fenestration—no gable roofs and cupolas.

In the case of two prototype dormitories at the University of Texas and the University of Houston, much of the money saved on the basic structure was plowed back into the interiors in the form of private or semi-private baths, wall-to-wall carpeting, year-round air conditioning, and so forth. Some of these "extravagances" actually produced economies in construction, operation, or maintenance—but not enough to offset the cost of the lounges, study halls, dining facilities, maid service, counseling staff, and other special features included in these particular packages.

As a result, the prototype dormitories cost as much to build as the average residence hall, and about twice the average to live in. An associate of O'Meara's argues that "you get what you pay for"—that is, the extra amenities and services are worth the extra cost of room and board. The school that wants to provide housing within its students' means as well as its own, however, will derive more comfort from the implications of the financing arrangements O'Meara-Chandler is now offering.

From the point of view of cost, the most comforting of the three plans is a proposal by which the firm will build a residence hall on the college's land, furnish it, and turn it over complete and ready for occupancy for a set price of $2,200 to $2,500 per student —no extras, no strings. At present, though, the most popular plan is the old stand-by: the off-campus dormitory which is built with the college's blessing and operated according to its regulations, but without entangling the college itself financially or administratively.

The third option is a lease-back arrangement under which a residence hall built on land the college deeds to the builder is leased back to the school for an annual rental equal to 8.46 per cent of the construction price of the building, the land and the building on it reverting to the school at the end of a 21-year lease.

Because the agreement does not describe the residence hall to be bought, only the terms on which the college can buy it, the plan offers the school an opportunity to specify what physical facilities it wants and can afford under the terms of the lease, although the college must exercise its control over the proposed building and its pricetag within the framework set up by a predetermined structural system.

But if flexibility is the criterion, it is better met by arrangements like the one now being offered by a Chicago firm, appropriately named A.I.D. (American Institutional Development) Corporation, which extends "nothing down, 12 years to pay" financing to any residence hall constructed by any system. There are only two stipulations: the college must submit plans of the proposed building for the corporation's approval, and it must demonstrate that it can pay the annual rental—usually about one-tenth of the construction cost of the building. Otherwise, the agreement follows the usual pattern: the corporation builds the residence hall on the college's land, leases it back to the college for the 12-year period required to amortize its initial cost, and then turns the building over to the lessee.

One of A.I.D.'s first customers will be Parsons College, which will use the lease-back arrangement to finance one of its new upperclass houses. As President Roberts is the first to point out, Parsons is the last college to need such a program. "I just want to show it can be done," he maintains. "It won't do anything for us that we're not doing for ourselves—but it could save 500 other colleges from dying."

The question is whether these schools can pay the price of salvation. Lease-back arrangements and similar schemes for private financing are the collegiate version of installment buying, and the debate over whether the college can afford them promises to rage as long and loud as the debate over whether the consumer can afford the easy credit that has become the backbone of his way of life.

Many colleges are in much the same position as a housewife who needs a washing machine, can't afford to send her laundry out, and can't stop doing the laundry until she saves the money to buy a machine outright. They know that a residence hall bought on a lease-back deal will cost them more in the long run than a similar building built by themselves and conventionally financed. (The entrepreneurs of education are not philanthropists, although the tax benefits on short-term depreciable investments make it unnecessary for them to be usurers either.) But the colleges need housing badly, and they often lack the capital or credit to buy it under conventional

financing arrangements. For such colleges, housing provided immediately, with no outlay of their strictly rationed capital and no call on their uncertain credit, may be worth its undeniably high cost to their students— or, more often, to themselves.

Nevertheless, most colleges are properly wary of rushing down this sawdust trail to economic salvation. Every private financing scheme mentioned here, except the privately owned and operated residences that ask nothing of the college but its blessing and a steady supply of tenants, is based on the premise that the property will be amortized out of rental income —usually within 12 years after it goes up. The properties are therefore self-liquidating by definition, and the easy annual payment plan does nothing to ameliorate the painful symptoms that so often afflict the self-amortizing project: high charges to the student, construction that is cheap and shows it, or both.

President Roberts of Parsons College bases his advocacy of A.I.D. Corporation's lease-back plan, and similar arrangements which assume amortization out of income, on his own conviction that the student, not the college, should pay for housing. This position is being taken by a growing number of expert observers of the peculiar economics of higher education, but few colleges have put the theory into prac-

tice. Some hesitate because they feel that higher room rents would drive away tuition-paying students or incense parents and alumni. More often, though, they simply disagree with the theory, because they have come to believe that the residence hall is an integral part of the educational plant. To them, expecting student rentals to cover the cost of building a new residence hall is as absurd as expecting laboratory fees to cover the construction cost of a new science building.

LIVE AND LEARN

Living in any dormitory teaches the student something. It is up to the college to decide what it wants him to learn there, and plan the building accordingly. It may choose simply to create an environment which is hospitable to unstructured learning—bull sessions, browsing in the library, or conversation around the coffee pot. It may emphasize the intellectual and cultural, as well as the academic, aspects of college life by encouraging informal associations between older and younger scholars, or by simply making art and books and music accessible, if not actually unavoidable. Or it may use the dormitory to supplement or reinforce the academic program, making the dormitory partner to the classroom as in the new housing

at Michigan State, making the dormitory itself the classroom as in Stephens College's West Hall, or making the dormitory the locus of a variety of learning aids—from tutors to television to teaching machines.

From this point of view, the concerted attack on costs seems merely a detour from the main path to more productive student housing. Yet the strands that compose the pattern of student housing are so closely interwoven that a change in any one inevitably affects others. If a college strives to increase the social amenity of a residence hall, physical amenities almost always follow. If it proposes to provide physical amenities, in spite of the cost, it finds that many of them are not only feasible but economical. In the same way, schools which accept a helping hand from the entrepreneurs of college housing may find that the economic expedient can also bring within their reach many of the amenities characteristic of the educationally oriented living environment.

For in spite of all the pressures to produce more and more housing faster and faster, the American college is not indulging in expediency for its own sake. The expedients it resorts to fall, for the most part, well within the scope of Webster's first definition: "suitable means to accomplish an end." And since the end is education, excellence is the first expedient.

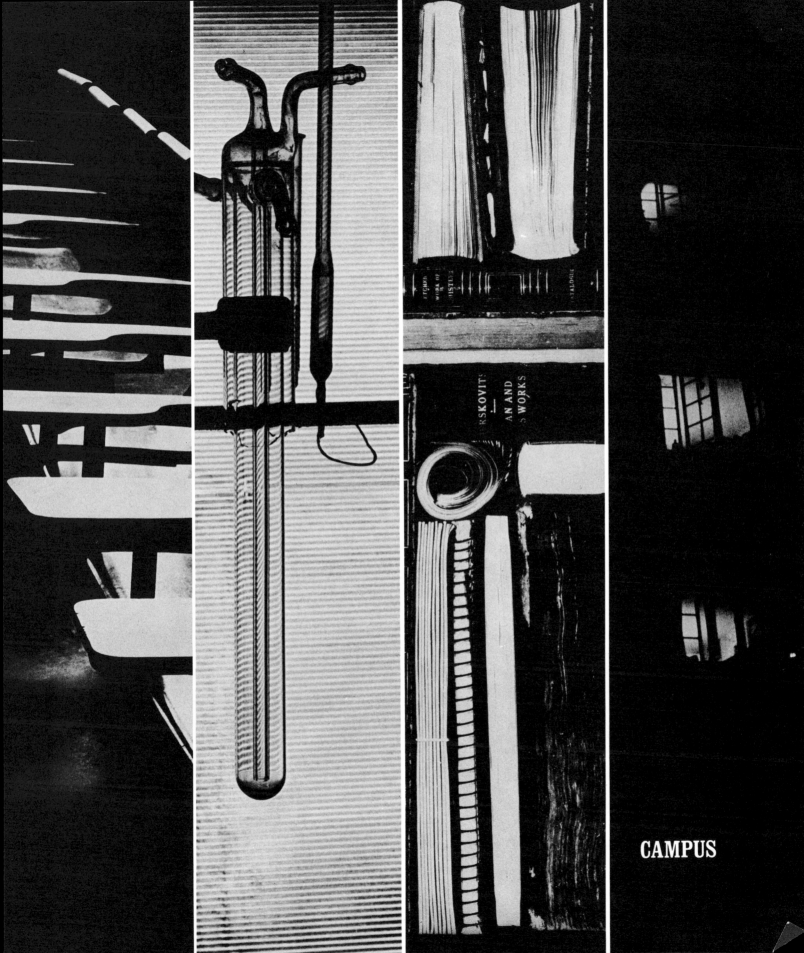

CAMPUS

EDUCATION

A college or university is more than the total of the elements (human and real estate) that comprise it. It is a place, a culture, a road to the future, and a pathway from the past. What happens to the student during his years of college may result more from his interaction with his peers and his faculty than from the course content of his classes. Part of what happens reflects the physical environment.

The extent to which a campus contributes to the institution's purposes, the efficiency and economy with which it functions, often are more the result of planning than of the design of individual buildings. Planning a college or university is a far more complex process than most persons, even those directly involved, realize.

CAMPUS
by
James J. Morisseau

"A college or university today provides in its complexity most of the elements, frustrations, and confusion of an urban society," commented Walter A. Netsch, Jr., of Skidmore, Owings and Merrill, who has had an opportunity to confront the problem of campus planning in a number of places. The campus is like a city because it is the focus of the lives of those around it. A great variety of people on or near it work, play, visit, eat, acquire goods and services, and drive cars to the campus. In short, it has none of the nice simple qualities of single-purpose developments like suburbs and industrial parks. Lawrence Lackey, a California planner, observed that an enrollment of 25,000 plus faculty and staff and their families, plus the pop-

ulation needed to serve a community of this size, produces a total population in and around the campus of about 92,000.

As James W. Clark, campus planner for Ohio State University, has pointed out, there are all kinds of students: male and female; undergraduate and graduate; fraternity and independent; professional and technical; day and night; full-time and part-time; credit and noncredit; residential and commuter. They cover the full spectrum of ages, races, creeds, and national origins. Faculty members may be full-time or part-time, and some hold full-time or consulting jobs in business or industry. Others may be involved in contract research. When divided along disciplinary lines or according to academic rank, they represent a wide variety of interests that are often in conflict. Then, there is the administrative hierarchy, starting with the president and running down to the maintenance men.

And there is a constant stream of visitors: convention and conference goers, prospective students, parents, alumni, sports fans, music and art lovers, congressmen, state and local politicians, and, not least, the institution's trustees. All of these people must be transported to and from the campus and through it. Many of them must be fed. Some of them must be housed. Others must find on or near the campus places to worship, to study, to relax, to play. On campuses outside the city, they must be able to purchase a range

of goods and services nearly as wide as that required by a city population. And, ideally, all of this should happen in surroundings that are amenable to the institution's primary purposes, education and research.

In short, the campus administration must concern itself with all of the city's myriad problems on a smaller scale—transit, traffic, housing, zoning, utilities, health and sanitation, law enforcement, recreation, and, of course, the development of the surrounding area. And all this must be done from the framework of the college as a cultural and intellectual center of our society.

The lifetime of a college and university "must be measured in centuries and you must expect change," according to Herbert H. Swinburne. Mr. Swinburne, who is handling the expansion plan at Temple University, maintains that the planner must look back 20 years and forward no less than 30. Some of his colleagues hold out for a plan ranging anywhere from 20 to 50 years ahead. But Mr. Swinburne and his colleagues stress that detailed planning be limited to the first 10 years or so. Beyond that the future ought to be sketched out in broad strokes rather than in specifics.

Their reasoning is plausible enough. No one, they argue, can predict with any accuracy what will be happening in the educational program several decades from now. Therefore, no one can effectively arrange rooms, buildings and outdoor spaces to accommodate that program.

One obvious answer is to design campus buildings to allow for changes in function over the years. Experience shows us that such changes occur in any event. Ohio State found this out when it recently converted office space into classrooms in a building that started out 50 years before as a chemistry laboratory. Building on such examples, many of the architects and planners now working on campuses are planning buildings to make transitions simpler, less painful, and less expensive. Planning for change is even more important now in an era of rapid transition and growth. Four-year liberal arts colleges are showing a tendency to grow into complex universities, with a broad range of departmental and research activities. Teachers colleges are being converted into liberal arts colleges. Two-year community colleges, intended in part to satisfy some of the demand for vocational and technical training, have proliferated. But many of them have been forced to neglect vocational programs to handle the flood of students who plan to transfer to four-year institutions for liberal arts degrees. Others have changed character entirely and have evolved into four-year institutions themselves. At least one has become a full-fledged university.

And, of course, the changing nature of American society itself places additional burdens on the campus planner. One of the most troublesome is the commuting student and his automobile. As Mr. Netsch put the latter problem: "Campuses originally pedestrian in nature now resemble urban parking lots with buildings."

Long-range planning would seem to be the only hope if chaos is to be avoided on the campus. Many educators have reached this conclusion and acted accordingly. But the evidence is that the majority are not planning either comprehensively enough or far enough into the future to meet the needs of their institutions or of the nation.

Some are not planning at all.

"We don't know where we're going," said one unusually candid president, "but we're on our way."

Still others have not taken the trouble to find out where they stand. Dr. John X. Jamrich, Assistant Dean of the College of Education, Michigan State University, maintained in an earlier EFL report that, before embarking on a building program, colleges ought to have established enrollment projections, conducted curriculum studies, and analyzed the adequacy and utilization of the existing plant.

Dr. Jamrich surveyed the planning activities of 124 small liberal arts colleges in the Midwest and outlined the results in the EFL report: *To Build or Not to Build: A Report on the Utilization and Planning of Instructional Facilities in Small Colleges*. He found that only 12 of the institutions studied had undertaken intensive total studies. Twenty-nine had no studies planned; 44 had only enrollment projections; 28, only curricular studies; 11, studies of plant adequacy and utilization.

Another study, undertaken in 1961 by the management consulting firm of Booz, Allen and Hamilton, of Chicago, pointed up the colleges' failure to look to the future. Dr. H. L. Wilsey, Partner-in-Charge of the firm's Educational Administration Division, reported that, of 831 different colleges and universities responding to a survey, 59 per cent had future plans of some kind, 33 per cent were developing plans, and 8 per cent had no plans at all.

The crucial discovery was that less than half the institutions were making plans that extended more than five years into the future.

"Indications are," Dr. Wilsey said, "that quite a few institutions laying claim to long-range planning were only in the very early stages of planning."

At the same time, there was a wide range in the planning areas covered by the various institutions in the survey. Some 82 per cent had plans for future enrollments, but less than three-quarters had plans pertaining to operating budgets, instructional programs, fund raising, or community services.

On the assumption that the 831 surveyed institutions, representing 45 per cent of the national total, were typical of all American colleges and universities, Dr. Wilsey estimated that current planning would provide seats for less than 70 per cent of the additional stu-

dents expected on the campus in 1970 under then-current projections.

"In other words," he said, "although it is expected that 3,000,000 additional young people will be seeking college training by 1970, the present plans of existing American colleges and universities will accommodate at most an additional 2,000,000 by that time."

The conclusion appears to be borne out in large measure by the colleges' own reports to the Office of Education on planned dollar expenditures for new facilities between 1961 and 1965. These indicate the colleges plan to spend about $1.2 billion a year, in contrast to the estimated $1.9 billion required to meet enrollment demands.

Dr. Wilsey found that most of the comprehensive, long-range planning now under way is being carried on by the larger institutions, most of them publicly supported. Smaller, privately supported institutions usually find it difficult to finance long-range planning. Donors prefer to buy buildings, not piles of paper and drawings.

THE ANATOMY OF A PLAN

Planning is a complex and an expensive process. Southern Illinois University, for example, paid the St. Louis architectural firm of Hellmuth, Obata and Kassabaum $100,000 to create a master plan for its new center at Edwardsville. Months of conferences with leading educators and cultural

experts, and with the faculty and administration, took place before a single line was drawn on paper. Similar expenditures of time and money went into other planning jobs investigated in preparation for this report. What was accomplished; just what goes into a master plan?

Dr. Wilsey maintains that the institution must first arrive at its own understanding of the over-all goals of higher education in terms of educational philosophy and national needs. Then, it must determine its role in the total picture.

Here, the college must decide how many students it will take, and what kind of students. Will it accept all comers so long as they hold a high school diploma? Or will it be selective and, if so, how selective? Will it limit its offerings to a four-year liberal arts program? Will it offer vocational technical programs? Graduate work? Professional programs? Adult education? How much of the responsibility of the home, the church, community organizations, and the future employer will it assume in educating its students? To what extent will it maintain research activities in the effort to contribute to new knowledge? What other services will it provide to the community? Will it be a residential college, a commuter institution, or both?

The educational objectives then are translated into specific programs. The academic planners spell out what degrees will be offered and the courses of study leading to them. Then the academic organization is established as a coherent system of schools, colleges, departments (if there are to be such), research units, institutes, and service organizations. The academic calendar—the semester plan, trimester, or quarter system—is adopted, and the length of the academic week and day established.

At this stage, projections are made of the enrollment expected (in the case of institutions required to take all comers) or desired at each stage of development. The analysis indicates the enrollments at each academic level and, if possible, a breakdown by sex and marital status.

From these projections, faculty and staff needs can be determined. At this point in the planning study, the faculty shortage or economic considerations may prompt the planners to re-examine their earlier decisions about the variety of course offerings and the nature of the academic organization. More restricted offerings and new teaching methods may result in more effective use of available faculty.

The next step is to outline the facilities required at each stage of development based on enrollment and staff projections. The requirements are broken down by function: instructional; general, including administration, auditorium, chapel, stadium, and the like; auxiliary, including the student union, cafeteria, and infirmary; research; residential; and site, including outdoor recreation spaces, parking, utilities, and general landscaping.

Here, the physical dimensions of the campus begin to become apparent. In the instructional area, the average college or university has about 175 square feet of space per student. But it has been suggested that, with more efficient utilization, 125 square feet should be adequate.

Walter Netsch calls for the allocation of 150 square feet per undergraduate student, 200 square feet per graduate student, 235 square feet of housing for each resident student (substantially more for married students), and 300 square feet of parking and maneuvering area per auto permitted on campus. Others suggest that the library ought to seat half the student body at one time.

Figures such as these can be translated into total floor area requirements. From these findings, rough cost estimates can be made.

Sam B. Zisman, planner and architect from San Antonio, Texas, who is developing plans for Skidmore College, in Saratoga Springs, New York, argued that the campus actually has five dimensions: length, width, height, time, and cost.

The dimension of cost is a difficult one for the private institutions, Mr. Zisman said, because most donors and even some college planners fail to recognize that the cost of placing a new building on campus involves much more than construction of the building itself. Furniture and equipment, a share of the development cost of related campus facilities, such as park-

ing, roads, water mains, and utilities, and the cost of site development and landscaping must be taken into account.

He estimated, for example, that it will cost roughly $1 million to construct a new library at Skidmore, but that the total cost, not including books, will come to more than $1,350,000.

"That $350,000," he added, "is the hardest kind of money to get."

Once determined, these dimensions can be translated into a graphic presentation, a schematic, preliminary master plan. This plan, on which the elements of the campus are laid out in hypothetical fashion, helps the planners to identify what buildings are needed in first-stage construction and to come up with rough predictions of the buildings involved in later stages and their timing. At the same time, cost estimates can be made for each stage. It also helps determine the general nature of a site that would be adequate for development of the campus.

Site selection itself is another complicated and sometimes painful process. Different communities tend to compete for the honor (and economic advantages) of providing a home for a new college or university. Political pressures are not uncommon. Even without them, the job is time-consuming. Eighty-four sites were inspected, 12 of them in detail, before one was chosen for the University of California campus at Santa Cruz.

Size is the most obvious requirement in choosing a site, but even that is a relative question. The University of California has set 1,000 acres as the minimum for its new, 27,500-student campuses, all of which are in more or less rural settings.

In contrast, the new University of Illinois campus in Chicago will encompass only 106 acres, and its academic core, only 40 acres.

The planners must be concerned with the shape of the site, the nature of the terrain, subsoil conditions, and natural hazards such as floods and earthquakes. The climate, and even the microclimate, can be decisive. Official site selection criteria for the new University of California campuses require planners to avoid locations in the path of known "smog rivers."

The campus must be reasonably accessible by auto, bus, rail, air, and, in some cases, rapid transit. On the other hand, it should obviously not be bisected by a railroad or heavily travelled highway. The University of Arkansas has such a severe transportation problem it has purchased its own aircraft to shuttle university officials to and from campus on business trips. Water, sewage disposal, and utilities must be provided for.

The site should not be surrounded by urban blight, heavy industry, or, as the University of California has found, under or near an airport approach path. In studying all these problems, planners prepare detailed circulation and access maps, land-use maps, and diagrams of utility lines for each proposed site.

Sometimes, the existence of a cultural or scientific institution will influence the planners in the choice of a site. The site of New College, a would-be southern outpost of the Ivy League, for example, adjoins that of the state-owned Ringling Museum in Sarasota, Florida. The museum contains one of the outstanding collections of art in the South. The Asolo Theatre, the only original eighteenth century Italian theater in America, is on the museum grounds. The walls at either side of the grounds will be torn down and the museum and theater, though still state-owned, will become an integral part of the campus. The theater will be used for student productions. The site for the new University of California at San Diego was largely determined by the location of the Scripps Institute of Oceanography near La Jolla.

When a site is selected, careful plans are drawn to fix the circulation patterns for automobiles and pedestrians, the location of utilities, and the types of buildings that will be placed on different parts of the campus.

Here, the planners must tackle several crucial problems. The circulation plan is one of the most difficult. Mixing people and automobiles is as difficult on a campus as anywhere else.

Then there is the question of zoning. How shall the various elements of the campus be put together? The tendency has been to designate one zone as the academic core, restricted to the instructional process and contact between students and faculty. Another

zone is set aside for residential purposes and limited pretty much to students. The last is the "activity" zone, where the student, the faculty, and the public come together for athletic and cultural events or as part of the administrative process. In some cases, separate zones, and even separate "campuses," are designated for varsity athletics, research, and other facilities. Whether the development of such separate zones is beneficial to the institution's aims is a debatable question.

Landscape architecture—the placement of roads, walks, parking lots, and play fields, and the creation of large and small outdoor spaces between buildings—is as important in establishing a campus atmosphere as the exterior design and interior arrangement of buildings. A screen of shrubbery and a judiciously placed bench can create an excellent outdoor space for study, small student gatherings, or even outdoor classes. Carefully planted trees can screen low buildings against the sun and cut air-conditioning costs, or screen one campus zone from another. The landscape architect generally is responsible for grading, drainage, irrigation, roads and walks, walls and steps, and plantings of trees, grass, and shrubbery. What he does originally, seldom is repeated or changed; his work has a lasting influence on the evolution of the campus. His decisions affecting the circulation and service elements of the plan can serve as the pivotal considerations around which the determination of building sites are made.

NEW PLANS FOR OLD CAMPUSES

At this point, it seems appropriate to look at the planning process on existing campuses. There are no basic differences in principle. The objectives —a well-ordered, efficient plant and an atmosphere conducive to the academic process—are the same. But an existing institution embarking on an expansion plan has a different set of problems.

It has a campus around which community development probably already has taken place. Unlike a new institution, it cannot go out and find an ideal site, and it usually finds it difficult (if not indeed impossible) because of land values, to alter the size and shape of the existing site.

The college has a collection of existing buildings, some of which are old and inefficient. Others may be newer, more efficient, but in the wrong place.

It has a faculty and a set of traditions and administrative habits. Changes in the educational program or new methods and procedures that would step up efficiency are difficult to impose. It has alumni, who may resist changes in the campus as they knew it. It may or may not have a previously drawn master plan.

In the planning process these factors must be taken into account. The first step usually is to create a planning committee representing the administration, faculty, heads of specialized units, and the trustees. The committee attempts to set directions in which all or a majority of interested parties will concur. But final decisions must be left to a single authority, usually the president and sometimes the business officer, subject to approval by the trustees if policy matters are involved.

The committee, often with the aid of special faculty subcommittees, reviews the institution's objectives and undertakes a review of the educational program and curriculum. It may suggest reforms and improvements in both areas. Enrollment projections or a decision as to ultimate enrollment then are made. Determination of ultimate enrollment should always be made with true humility, since such decisions are normally revised by each generation of trustees and administrators.

Planners and consultants then undertake an intensive analysis (usually in map form) of the existing plant, grounds, circulation elements, utilities, and the neighborhood surrounding the campus to determine their adequacy for the new program. Buildings are studied to determine whether they require replacement or renovation or if their location blocks effective planning for expansion. Utilization of all building spaces is studied to determine if expansion can be achieved through more efficient use patterns. (Dr. Jamrich found, in studying some 60 small liberal arts colleges for his EFL report, that enrollments could be increased by 50 per cent without erecting a new instructional building, if the factor of obsolescence was ignored.)

A new master plan then is drawn, setting forth by stages the new buildings required, necessary renovation projects, buildings to be destroyed, changes in circulation and utility patterns, and other improvements.

Expansion need not be limited to the old campus. It may even involve its abandonment. Mr. Zisman pointed out that expansion can take four forms: an increase in the type of facilities already there; duplication through the addition of separate graduate or professional schools on the campus; duplication through the creation of a co-ordinate or satellite campus; or relocation, the creation of an entirely new campus on another site.

Examples of simple expansion and the addition of graduate and professional schools are legion. MacMurray College in Jacksonville, Illinois, a liberal arts college for women, chose to open a co-ordinate college for men close to the original campus. St. John's College, in Annapolis, Maryland, is planning to duplicate itself on a satellite campus in Santa Fe, New Mexico. And Skidmore College is abandoning its old campus in downtown Saratoga Springs, New York, in favor of an entirely new plant on the outskirts of town.

The last solution, Mr. Zisman notes, need not be more expensive than the decision to rebuild and remodel an old campus. His study of four colleges that chose to move is reported in the EFL report: *New Campuses for Old: A Case Study of Four Colleges That Moved.*

147

EVERY SCHOOL MUST HAVE ITS BELL

It is not clear whether the planners are responsible or whether the problems that led the colleges to employ them are the motive force—but *the campus is changing*. It is taking on new patterns, and its buildings are assuming new shapes.

Only one campus phenomenon seems to remain unaffected. A century ago, Ezra Cornell wrote of his dream for the university that bears his name:

"There was also in my dream another special feature, which no one has as yet attempted to realize—a lofty campanile — a clock tower looking proudly down the slope, over the traffic of the town, and bearing a deep-toned peal of bells."

Last year, when Edward Durell Stone unveiled the model of his plan for the new State University campus at Albany, New York, university officials noticed to their surprise that a tall, slim tower had been placed at one corner of the central mall. One official, remembering that such a tower had not been discussed in earlier planning conferences, asked what it was doing there. Mr. Stone's explanation:

"Every school must have its bell."

At the new University of California campus at Irvine, planner William L. Pereira will develop a lush park with a lake at its center. The park will provide a symbol for the campus that will be in striking contrast to the dry, brown Southern California terrain around it.

Florida Presbyterian College, in Tampa, and St. Andrews Presbyterian College, in Laurinburg, N. C., were designed by different architects, Charles W. Brubaker of Perkins and Will, Chicago, and A. G. Odell, Jr. and Associates, of Charlotte, N. C., respectively. But both will have as their symbol a chapel. Both chapels will be located on causeways joining two parts of the campus across an artificial lake.

Caudill, Rowlett and Scott, in developing a master plan for Ohio State University, decided that the Olentangy River ought to become its symbol . . . Everywhere there is the conviction that every great campus has a symbol. Possibly now, with change so much a part of campus life, the need for a changeless symbol is more important than it ever has been.

FORMAL OR INFORMAL

Most planners have concluded that the informal campus plans have survived better than the monumental, rigidly formal designs. Walter Netsch cited Harvard as an example of the informal and successful, and the University of Virginia as a case of the formal and less successful. Most of today's planners have taken the cue and lean toward the informal campus layout.

However, they still tend toward rigid zoning in an effort to separate the academic, "activity," and residential areas of the campus. The effort now is to plan the campus so that each function can expand within its own zone.

One solution to this problem is the system of "thru-site campus zones" developed by Caudill, Rowlett and Scott. However, some observers have suggested that this insistence on rigid zoning may be among the many preconceptions upon which planners have proceeded that do not in fact prove to be true. It is possible, it was argued, to intermix facilities successfully on small campuses and on those which plan little growth without creating problems. Such intermixture may very well contribute to the creation of a far more integrated campus culture than the careful zoning of various aspects of collegiate life into neat planning packages. Harvard was cited as a case where various facilities have been intermixed with success.

The campus is beginning to lose its excessively open character through both design and necessity. Some planners have heeded those critics of city planning who argue that a variety of comparatively small, open spaces between buildings is perhaps more desirable than large spaces that create excessive distances between buildings and a disconnected, suburban-type campus. Intensive development of the site is no longer regarded as something to be shunned by all but big city institutions.

At the Albany campus of the State University of New York, for example, Mr. Stone has gone to the extreme of putting all academic facilities for a campus of 10,000 under one roof, seven blocks long by three blocks wide.

Four residence complexes, located close by, include dormitory towers that are 22 stories high. This tight complex will sit in the middle of a 300-acre site, a former golf course.

In most instances, the trend seems to be toward the development of a rather tight academic core, with housing, "activities," and other functions growing out from it. At the heart or focal point of the core, there is a new tendency to place lecture hall facilities. At both the University of Illinois in Chicago and the new State University at Albany, the roof of the lecture hall will form huge open plazas that will be the crossroads of the campus. Mr. Netsch created an open-air amphitheater by depressing the center of the mall and created four other natural meeting places for students at the corners of the mall.

The lecture hall, in these instances, is displacing the library as the focal point of the campus. The library joins a group of structures around the lecture facility that include the student union and, in some cases, the administration building.

California, however, seems to be bucking the trend toward the tight, centralized campus. There, plans call for the division of two of the State's newest campuses into a series of residential colleges surrounding an academic downtown that will contain major academic, activity, and administrative facilities.

At San Diego, 12 colleges, of 2,000 to 2,500 students each, will be estab-

lished in clusters of 4. Each college will have its own residential, instructional, and recreational facilities and each cluster, according to current planning, will have a gymnasium and probably a library. Such university-wide facilities as the main library, auditorium, and administration building will be located downtown.

A similar concept, but one in which the residential colleges would be more dispersed than at San Diego and where there will be more stress on actual instruction in the residences, has been proposed for the new Santa Cruz campus.

These developments obviously turn their back on the concept of rigid separation of housing and academic zones. They put an end to the problem of the "academic Levittowns," where the "work" of education tends to be put aside when the student leaves the academic area for his home in the residential suburb.

And the residential college idea tends to avoid the problems encountered by planners of centralized institutions in trying to maintain the "10-minute campus." This concept, based on the traditional 50-minute class session and 10-minute break, requires that it take no more than 10 minutes to walk between any two points in the academic core, allowing time to climb stairs or ride elevators.

Anton J. Egner, Assistant to the President at Cornell University, concluded in a thesis published in 1962 that in an ideal campus layout, the 10-

minute campus could accommodate an enrollment of 32,500 students. Ideal conditions never prevail, and many sprawling state and private institutions with much smaller enrollments have difficulty maintaining the 10-minute class change.

The San Diego residential colleges will have three-minute campuses. Theoretically, they could be reproduced innumerable times, assuming they were academically self-sufficient. Available land, and not enrollment, would become the limiting factor in determining ultimate size. In practice, California has set an enrollment limit of 27,500 for each of its university campuses.

On the big university campuses, with their collection of graduate and professional schools, the trend has been toward the arrangement of both graduate and undergraduate facilities so that related disciplines are close to each other. The new Ohio State plan calls for a grouping of the specialized schools around a social sciences and humanities core. Education, business studies, social work, and law are within the core area. Engineering, the physical sciences, and mathematics are grouped on one side of it. And botany and zoology, dentistry, medicine, pharmacy, the biological sciences, veterinary medicine, and agriculture are strung out in a rather logical sequence on the other side. A similar pattern is being followed at UCLA and the new University of California campus at Irvine.

Under this pattern, space still is being designated by discipline. There is a physics building, or buildings, a history building, a languages building, a biological sciences building, and so forth. But within the pattern, the planners are attempting to get more flexibility, to design spaces that can easily be converted to other uses. At Irvine, for example, a standard bay system will be employed in all buildings so that functions within them can be rearranged. The use of spaces, Mr. Pereira said, may not be designated until after the buildings are completed.

Other planners are going a step further and providing space by function rather than by discipline. The outstanding examples are Walter Netsch's University of Illinois Chicago campus and Gyo Obata's campus for Southern Illinois University at Edwardsville. Mr. Netsch, who has stressed the creation of a wide variety of spaces rather than convertibility, has placed all lecture space in a centrally located building. All regular classrooms are in their own buildings, all laboratories in laboratory buildings. All faculty offices and seminar rooms are located in a single, 28-story skyscraper.

At Edwardsville, Mr. Obata has designed separate buildings for classrooms and for laboratories, each with wings for faculty offices. To provide the greatest possible flexibility, he has taken all the "static" elements of a building—staircases, maintenance closets, washrooms, utility lines — and placed them in towers at the perimeter of the structure. This leaves clear, loft space for the "dynamic" elements—classrooms and laboratories — and it clears the way for their ready conversion to other uses. Architecturally, he has expressed the solution by sheathing the towers in brick and the buildings proper in precast concrete.

"FULL EMPLOYMENT" FOR THE CAMPUS

In assigning space by function and striving for convertibility, the planners are attempting to insure that new buildings or new campuses will be better utilized than most existing facilities. Nor are efforts to step up efficiency on existing campuses being ignored.

Computers have been put to work on the problem at MIT. In a project supported by a grant from EFL, the 7090 computer has been used to simulate a college—its students, faculty, instructional program, and available facilities. Last fall, it was used to schedule 20 different programs for each of 1,000 entering freshmen at MIT. Data preparation took three days but the actual scheduling job was done in eight minutes flat, at a total cost of less than 20 cents a student. Normal time for the job is eight man-weeks costing nearly $1.60 per student.

But the real advantages in the project, whimsically entitled GASP (for Generalized Academic Simulation Programs) may be in its potential use in testing the effects of program changes without subjecting the college to the risks and disruptions involved in trial runs. A change designed to improve utilization can be fed into the computer and placed in simulated operation. The actual effects of the change, including unforeseen problems, may be determined beforehand.

Elsewhere, colleges have turned to co-operative programs in an effort to make better use of such facilities as libraries, specialized laboratories, and gymnasiums, avoid duplication of courses that are sparsely attended, and obtain other economies possible through group effort.

Still other colleges are turning to year-round operation as a means of expanding enrollments without providing new facilities. Kalamazoo College, in Kalamazoo, Michigan, estimates that its new four-quarter calendar will help it to increase enrollments by as much as 66 per cent without putting up a single new building. Part of the increase will be made possible by a requirement that every student spend two to five credit-earning quarters in off-campus educational experiences, including at least one term abroad. The program is halfway through its second year, and, according to published academic results, is a success.

The trend to year-round programs or at least to a longer academic year has been followed by a growing acceptance of air conditioning as a necessary element in the design of college buildings.

Mr. Obata defended the use of air conditioning at the new Southern Illinois campus:

"Certainly it costs more to air-condition. But this university is designed for year-round use from 7 in the morning to 10 at night. You just have to air-condition in the (summer) weather we get in this area."

The University of California has adopted a statewide policy under which air conditioning is permitted if the "effective" temperature passes the discomfort point for the average person more than a certain number of days a year. The policy is liberal enough that 70 per cent of the building space at Irvine will be air-conditioned.

The State College system in California has gone a step further, authorizing air conditioning in "core-type" buildings — those in which economy is achieved by keeping perimeter walls to a minimum and having a good deal of interior, windowless space. Harry Harmon, chief of college facilities planning for the system, said that savings resulting from the core or block design of buildings justify the cost of air conditioning.

For some of the same reasons, the planners are shying away from the vast areas of glass that have been so popular in building design for the last 20 years. They have found that the build-up of temperature in buildings as the sun hits large glass surfaces has proven to be, as Mr. Evans, the California planner, put it, "the $64,000

question" in comfort control for academic facilities.

As a result, planners and architects have had to struggle with the problem of what to do about older buildings having too much glass in the wrong exposures, i.e.: on the south and west sides of a building. One answer has been to erect screens or sunshades of metal or concrete. Some new buildings have been designed with such screening, notably a new student union at UCLA. And a new dormitory at Temple University, designed by Nolen and Swinburne, has what amounts to a second wall of glass hung a few feet out from the side of the building.

Heat-absorbent grey glass is used in both the windows of the building and the screen. The result is that 60 to 75 per cent of heat and glare from the sun are dissipated.

THE VILLAIN WITH WHEELS

The war on the automobile and the effort to retain the pedestrian campus have imposed their own new patterns on campus design. Most common is the pattern of highway loops, one running the perimeter of the campus and, usually, a second circling the academic core. The loops, and an accompanying system of perimeter parking lots, reflect the planners' efforts to keep cars out of the academic core, thus achieving horizontal separation of auto and pedestrian traffic.

But, particularly in urban campuses, there is an effort to achieve vertical separation of the two types of traffic, something that long has been advocated for cities but never seriously tried. In Chicago, for example, Mr. Netsch has laid out a system of elevated pedestrian walkways running to the perimeter of the campus in four directions and converging at the plaza covering the lecture center. Limited truck and auto traffic then can be permitted into the campus at street level for deliveries and business purposes.

At Foothill College, Ernest Kump has taken advantage of hilly terrain to achieve vertical separation. All campus buildings are on two hilltops. All roads and parking areas are in the valleys, off the campus proper and out of sight.

An extreme answer was arrived at in Albany. There, Mr. Stone placed the entire academic complex on a podium one story off the ground. All pedestrian circulation is on the podium. All auto and truck traffic stops at the edges of the academic complex. Deliveries of supplies and equipment are handled by electric trucks in a tunnel system running under the podium.

Ohio State will employ variations of all these solutions in an attempt to handle the circulation problem on an existing campus. Perhaps its most dramatic move was to secure the relocation of a proposed expressway so the academic core would be unified and enlarged. The expressway will form part of the outer loop around the campus. An inner loop also will be created. Streets that now traverse the campus will be closed and converted into pedestrian malls. Only emergency vehicles will be permitted to enter.

At other points on the OSU campus, development plans call for the gradual creation of podium-type pedestrian plazas that will permit the movement and parking of autos below. The OSU plan is indicative of the near-insolubility of the parking problem on many campuses. Parking will be provided there in huge, open lots, in ramp-type parking garages, under buildings and elevated plazas, and underground. Nevertheless, the planners could find room for only 23,000 cars, the number estimated to be needed when the enrollment reaches 34,500 students. The projected top enrollment is 43,000, at which point 27,800 parking spaces will be needed.

Caudill, Rowlett and Scott pointed out that, to provide 27,800 spaces, 191 acres of open lots, or 10.4 million square feet of floor area in garages would be needed. The garage area would be the equivalent of converting all existing campus buildings for parking and adding another 2.9 million square feet. The cost of providing garage-type space, they added, would come to $50 million. They closed their argument on a hopeful note: better rapid transit might head off the need for 27,800 spaces.

It might be noted here that the University Facilities Research Center at the University of Wisconsin conducted a study of parking facilities under an EFL grant. The results indicated that, when the value of campus land reaches $3.50 to $4.50 a square foot, "it becomes advisable to consider construction of multi-level facilities rather than additional parking lots."

In some campuses, parking facilities are located so far from the academic core that transportation from parking lot to campus is required. Shuttle buses have been placed in service for this purpose on the University of Wisconsin campus. And the use of "elephant trains" has been suggested at other campuses. These are strings of passenger trailers hauled by small tractors, such as were used at both the New York and Seattle World's Fairs. They can be moved safely through pedestrian areas.

Elephant trains also have been suggested for use within the academic core at OSU, but the proposal has not yet been accepted by the University.

The planning effort at Michigan reflects the growing realization among campus planners that campus and urban problems are inseparable. Johnson, Johnson and Roy, who have worked on a redevelopment plan for Ann Arbor, also are handling planning studies for the University's Medical Center and the North Campus. One of their proposals has been the creation of a greenbelt of park lands following the river valley and a planned new link in the Interstate High-

way system. The belt would give the city much-needed open space and the university a natural link between campuses. The planners have proposed that the Medical Center be reoriented to face the greenbelt and river rather than downtown. The change, they said, would relieve traffic congestion in Ann Arbor as well as improving the Medical Center.

Michigan's problems in living with its community are minor compared to those of institutions in the big cities. The University of Chicago, for example, was plagued for years by conditions of urban blight, crime, and juvenile delinquency in the surrounding neighborhoods. Finally, the problem became so serious that the University assumed the leadership in what has become a concerted drive in cooperation with the city and state to rehabilitate the area under the Federal Urban Renewal program. In New York City, five colleges and universities joined recently to sponsor a nonprofit, co-operative housing project on the lower East Side.

Space is another crucial problem for these big city institutions. High real estate values have long since forced them into vertical expansion, the construction or purchase of high-rise buildings. In some cases, this has resulted in the loss of any feeling of campus. Some institutions, like Long Island University in Brooklyn, gain space through urban redevelopment projects. Northwestern University in Evanston, Illinois, will acquire 65 acres of land by filling in a section of the Lake Michigan shoreline. The cost is estimated at one-quarter that of purchasing land in Evanston. But, for others, the process has been more painful and more expensive.

Los Angeles City College, for example, went underground to build its electronics laboratories and engineering classrooms. St. Louis University will have an underground lecture center in a new science-engineering complex. The roof of the lecture center will serve as a pedestrian plaza, providing some open space on a crowded campus.

THE COLLEGE

The four previous chapters of this report deal with college housing, instructional space, laboratories, and libraries. These are the four largest areas of expenditure for colleges and the four most important. Put together they constitute less than two-thirds of the facilities expenditures for higher education, and they certainly do not constitute a complete college. Theaters, museums, recital halls, health centers, college unions, research facilities, art studios, trees, and many other types of facilities go into the making of a college campus. So do a number of less tangible things such as tradition, culture, intellectual environment, and the visual delight that a campus can provide.

Americans are an introspective people, and almost all aspects of our life have come under scrutiny in this generation, as indeed they should in a democratic society. Among those aspects of life which have received intensive study from all sides is the campus.

It is a foregone conclusion among those who have studied the American college that the three major factors which influence the graduating student are: first, what kind of a person he was when he came to college; second, the total impact of the college environment on him, particularly his relationship to his peers and his faculty; and third, his formal course work in college.

In planning and replanning our campuses it is vital to bear in mind that we are shaping buildings which will themselves shape the lives of students and faculty members who will be occupying them for the better part of a century to come.

What happens to America will in large part be determined by our developed intellect in the coming years, and this will depend largely on our colleges.

What kinds of places they are, what intellectual accomplishments and attitudes and values they develop, will depend largely on students and faculty. But they will depend in part on the kinds of physical environment we provide for them.

RENOVATIONS

New buildings are not necessarily the only answer to campus development. In many cases, old buildings can be converted or renovated to serve the educational process for many more years. In fact, the imaginative remodeling of old buildings often offers substantial advantages over the erection of new ones.

Take what happened in Brooklyn: Long Island University acquired the most ornate basketball court in the world by remodeling the orchestra floor of the old Brooklyn Paramount Theatre (overleaf and this page). It is estimated that the renovation cost was one-tenth the cost of erecting a new gymnasium. As a bonus, the university got four new lecture halls by remodeling the theater's upper balcony.

In Philadelphia, a musty furniture warehouse was transformed into classroom, laboratory, and other academic space for the students of Drexel Institute of Technology. The job, which took 15 months, was completed in the spring of 1963.

Like many landlocked urban institutions, Drexel had been caught in the pinch between needed space and missing dollars. It had to expand, but urban congestion made building sites either unavailable or prohibitively expensive.

Then, Drexel acquired the Red Lion Storage Warehouse and, after an EFL-financed study, decided to renovate rather than tear it down. The savings amounted to nearly a half-million dollars and occupancy took place more than a half-year

157

sooner than would have been possible if the building were razed and a new one erected in its place.

The old warehouse, a loft building 50 feet wide by 200 feet long, included more than 78,000 square feet of space. That space has been converted, economically, into 33 classrooms, 6 labs, 6 seminar rooms, 3 research areas, a computer laboratory, a reference reading room, a faculty lounge, and 46 offices.

The full story of Drexel's decision to renovate and the considerations behind it is told in EFL's report, Space and Dollars: An Urban University Expands.

Renovation also can mean new life for outmoded campus buildings. Harvard, for example, opened a new language study center in 1959 in a building that then was more than 100 years old. (See photos this page and overleaf.)

Boylston Hall had been built in 1858 as a chemistry laboratory, anatomical museum, and library. Over the years, the building was added to and changed in function to house a history library, an Oriental Institute, and psychology laboratories. But the new renovation job involved a complete transformation of the building, both in function and interior appearance. The structure was gutted and, where once there had been four floors of space, five complete floors and a mezzanine floor were installed. New wiring made possible the installation of the most up-to-date electronic equipment for language instruction.

Other institutions have completed or are planning even more imaginative renovation projects. At West Virginia University, an engineering study indicated that a retractable roof could be erected over one end of the football stadium to provide a field house and basketball court for little more than half the cost of a separate structure. The Syracuse University master plan includes a proposal that, after a new stadium is built, the existing one be converted into a three-level parking garage for 2,700 cars.

As the experience of these institutions indicates, the colleges would do well to look twice at their old buildings before deciding to tear them down. To spare the wrecker's axe may be to spare the budget. A good rule of thumb may be to renovate if the building is where it belongs, is structurally sound, and possesses beauty, however ancient. If the building is in the wrong place, if its interiors are practically unchangeable, if it is ugly, abandon it.

161

BRICKS AND MORTARBOARDS : CONCLUSION

This book sets forth the difficult *physical* problems that beset American colleges and universities today, the far tougher physical problems looming just ahead, and an array of imperative reforms. The problems are staggering in mass and bewildering in detail. Onrushing developments define the challenge and demand response. The future begins next September.

CHALLENGE

EXPLOSIVE GROWTH

Over 4,000,000 degree-credit students are now enrolled in our colleges and universities. This figure will double by 1975: upwards of 8,500,000 students will then be enrolled. Somehow there is still no *real* appreciation of these figures even by the institutions of higher education themselves, much less by the general public. The projection has been repeated so often that it's become a commonplace. Perhaps the prospect is so outlandish that most of us—including, it would appear, many college presidents and trustees—plain don't believe it, even though recent experience has shown

that enrollment projections tend to understate the reality.

Moreover, the deluge is upon us already. By 1970—just seven years off—colleges and universities will have to make room for 7,000,000 students, almost 90 per cent more than they enroll now. Even more chilling is the fact that half the new applicants to college will pile up in the *next two years*. The wave of 1946-47 births will engulf the colleges next September. The lower schools underestimated this inexorable bulge at every level. There is no reason to believe that arithmetic will improve when the wave hits the colleges.

Are the colleges prepared? By no means. Institutional expansion plans fall 1,000,000 students (and $700 million a year) behind government projections of enrollment and needed expansion. Even today, faculty are scarce. College teachers for the first time in memory are enjoying a seller's market, as institutions bid against each other (and against business and government) for top talent. Can the colleges conceivably double their teaching staffs by 1975? Are they apt to build new facilities equal to twice all the campus facilities built in the three hundred years since Harvard was founded?

Growth in another area more than

matches the problem posed by doubling enrollment. This is the almost unbelievable proliferation of knowledge and information (and the physical means of their transmittal—books, pamphlets, periodicals). As Alvin Toffler points out in *Libraries,* the sheer quantity of information doubles every 10 years. This year's crop: 60,-000,000 pages of technical papers alone. How can this be stored, retrieved, disseminated?

CHANGE

Colleges can be sure that their enrollment will double within the decade, and that they will have to cope with double the amount of recorded information. But beyond these frightening certainties, all is speculation. Colleges and universities can be sure only that tremendous changes are in store that will affect every aspect of higher education. They have to build for change in their expansion.

Just as the population bulge is finally hitting the colleges, so the educational ferment now seething in the lower schools is bound to hit the colleges, too. Recent developments in the physical sciences and mathematics have all but transformed these sub-

163

jects in recent decades. Colleges now teach specialties unheard of 10 or 20 years ago. The humanities and the social sciences are being challenged and attacked from many points. The traditional departmentalization of college subjects, the old comfortable academic logrolling, can hardly withstand the pressures. Something—and probably quite a lot of things—will have to give.

Technology is finally reaching the educational backwaters. Will American colleges and universities be prepared to make wise use of television, tapes, computers, projectors, devices for storing and conveying information, electronic marvels still to be invented? On top of the technological challenge, colleges will confront inevitable change in the tried but no longer true ways of financing higher education. Can the private liberal arts institutions survive in anything like their present form in the face of rising costs? Can the state-supported universities, as they swell to monstrous size, combat the evils of mass education by creating campuses conducive to learning and individual development?

COMPLEXITY

The American pattern of higher education is past the understanding of foreign visitors, so diverse are the constituent institutions. We can hardly discern a pattern ourselves. Some-

thing called a college can be 80 students in an old resort hotel, or 2,000 students cloistered in ivy-covered Gothic on the eastern seaboard, or 20,000 students in an academic supermarket on the prairies, or 40,000 students on a high-rise island washed by big-city slums, or—any day, now—100,000 students in a multiversity.

Colleges are as plural as the American culture. One may be the greatest repository of culture in the Western world. Another, just as precious to an open society, may be a couple of hundred students and their teachers, held together by missionary zeal and a sense of impending bankruptcy.

If the over-all pattern is hard to grasp, equally complex in microcosm is the individual institution, especially the large-to-enormous university that will increasingly dominate the scene in higher education. Large or small, the institution must provide space for scores of very different purposes: instructional space that will accommodate the conventional lecture, the unknowable requirements of laboratory science, the needs of individual study; living space for faculty and student that will foster learning and not duplicate the "academic Levittowns" of the past; space for storing recorded knowledge and trying to keep abreast of its exponential growth rate; space for a whole array of educational facilities this book barely mentions—museums, theaters, health centers, college unions, research facilities . . . and trees.

"A college or university today provides in its complexity most of the elements, frustrations, and confusion of an urban society," says architect Walter Netsch. A medium-size institution with an enrollment of 25,000, say, equals a small city of 90,000 population or so, when you count in faculty and families plus the trade and service people (and their families) a community of this size requires. The campus has all the standard city problems to cope with—and even confined to *physical* problems, these are formidable. They include transit, traffic, housing, zoning, utilities, health and sanitation, law enforcement, recreation, area development. Take just traffic and transit, for instance. "Campuses originally pedestrian in nature now resemble urban parking lots with buildings," in the words of Mr. Netsch. An architectural rule-of-thumb allots 150 square feet per undergraduate student, 200 square feet per graduate student, but *300* square feet per campus automobile.

Campuses, like cities, must provide space and services for a heterogeneous population—students of all ages and varying status, faculty and families, the full range of administration from president to sweeper, and a constant stream of visitors—most of them on wheels. And this whole complex should be served with a grace that keeps paramount the essential purpose of the campus: the cultivation of the life of the mind.

RESPONSE

PLANNING

There is no universal pattern by which buildings and land can be pieced together to form an effective campus. The possible patterns are as many as the colleges themselves. But whatever the patterns and however they defy generalization, the colleges today have one thing in common: they are in transition and they must look deeply into the future. New forces beat upon them and raise new questions: the answers will influence the shape of college buildings and the campus for generations to come. Unhappily, it would be more accurate to say the answers *"should"* exert this influence. For there is scant evidence that the generality of colleges has come to grips with the kind of far-reaching, hard-headed, comprehensive planning that takes into account *everything* important that is happening or about to happen to higher education in America, and not just the gross pressure of doubled enrollments.

In the good old American tradition of bulling things through, the chances are that by hook or by crook we'll find room for 3,000,000 more college students in 1970, and another 1,500,-000 five years later. But as James Morisseau warns in his introduction to this book: "... unless there is better planning by the educators and a

greater financial commitment by society, there is danger that the needed facilities will be provided in a series of crash programs. Expediency rather than quality will be the byword. And our campuses will be crowded with misplaced academic slums, educationally self-defeating and a drain both educationally and economically on future generations."

To be sure, there are wide-ranging, imaginative campus plans being hammered out now, notably in California, Illinois, and New York State. But institutions in these states and a handful of others are the exception. Most educators are either making no plans at all, or plans entirely too limited in scope and time to meet the impending crisis ("We don't know where we're going, but we're on our way," the *Campus* chapter quotes one college president as saying with aplomb). A survey covering 45 per cent of all degree-granting institutions found that *less than half* had plans extending beyond five years. Even more serious than the shortsightedness of these plans is their narrow concentration on mere expansion, with little grasp of the dangers and opportunities that the future holds.

The colleges have too great a task before them to afford waste motion or costly, irreversible errors. To the extent that the physical environment helps shape the learning process, the future of American higher education—indeed, of the nation itself—depends on the outcome.

FLEXIBILITY

To meet pressing demands, campus space of all kinds—instructional, laboratory, residential—must be designed for maximum convertibility. Old-style dormitories must give way to housing that will make space for learning and amenities as well. Planners and designers, focusing on basic college purposes, must pay more heed to the social and psychological needs of the student, to more rewarding interaction between student and teacher, to the relative claims of solitude and community, to providing "a vigorously intellectual social climate." Colleges must provide instructional space of the greatest possible flexibility. It should meet needs ranging from the large lecture to individual study, and it should be readily convertible. Movable walls for year-to-year conversions, operable walls for immediate change will be the rule, not the exception, in instructional buildings.

To achieve comparable flexibility in buildings devoted to science is more difficult, but it can—and must—be done. The explosion of scientific knowledge makes yesterday's laboratory obsolete today. As the *Laboratories* chapter makes clear, pioneering efforts have proved that laboratories can be flexible and convertible, if the design deploys utilities and equipment so as not to freeze the pattern of walls and spaces. Soon it should be possible to convert a physics laboratory, almost overnight, into a biology laboratory.

Flexibility means many things. No college should brandish this stylish architectural catchword as a cure-all. Sound planning requires each college to think through the *kind* of flexibility that fits its particular character, expansion plans, and scientific orientation. Every institution must calibrate change and innovation with its own scale of values and foreseeable needs.

UTILIZATION

Closely bound up with the need for a flexible campus is the need for full utilization of campus space, time, people, and things. Flexible buildings mean that space can be readily adapted to use by large groups or small, depending on instructional needs. College space must do double or triple duty. Space for individual study will be provided in libraries or residences or in instructional buildings, or in all three.

Independent study will assume central importance in the emerging college of the future, especially in the larger institution. In part, this development will exploit a new maturity in the student, an increased recognition by educators of the power of self-teaching and its usefulness in shielding individual values from the tyranny of the group. In part, independent study is a form of *utilization*, whereby colleges will use scarce faculty and over-abundant students to greatest advantage. With teaching talent in short supply, we can no longer waste professors on mere exposition of facts. Increasingly, they will deal with values, concepts, the meaning of it all—in very large groups, or very small. More and more, students will get "the facts" from inanimate dispensers—books, films, tapes, television, and teaching machines—rather than from living teachers. Campus facilities, particularly the lecture hall and individual study spaces, must be adaptable to these new, technological carriers of knowledge.

Finally, the campus of the future must make far better use of *time*. Utilization of physical facilities is poor on many campuses, whether measured by the day, the week, or the season. It is not unreasonable for society to demand intensive use of expensive college facilities during more hours of the day and more weeks of the year than present convention affords. The college day will start earlier and end later. Saturday will appear on all calendars. The academic year will stretch to match the calendar year.

VISION

Above all, those who plan for America's colleges and universities must plan imaginatively, broadly, and with an open-mindedness that takes in an unpredictable future. They must build change itself into their plans.

The urgent needs of the future are upon us. But the sense of emergency must not foster expedient makeshifts at the cost of quality and grace and ultimate utility. The planners must look beyond the plethora of architectural and technical details. For the campus is much greater than the sum of its parts, whatever the talent and wisdom that inform the design of individual buildings. The campus as a whole must be framed for commodity, firmness, and delight. It must provide an environment that favors learning and understanding and intellectual interchange.

Campus architecture and design can help to reconcile the conflict between mass education and the individual, and to strike a balance between the economics of education and the human needs and values of the student.

This, at any rate, should be the vision.

CREDITS

Designed: Sutter and Wartik
Printed: Zabel Brothers, Inc.

OTHER REPORTS FROM EFL

The following publications are available from the offices of EFL: 477 Madison Avenue, N. Y. 22, N. Y.

ABOUT EFL
The purposes and activities of Educational Facilities Laboratories.

COLLEGE STUDENTS LIVE HERE.
A report on the what, why, and how of college housing; reviews the factors involved in planning, building, and financing student residences.

THE COST OF A SCHOOLHOUSE
A review of the factors contributing to the cost and effectiveness of school housing, including planning, building, and financing as well as the evolution of the schoolhouse and some conclusions about tomorrow's school.

DESIGN FOR ETV—Planning for Schools with Television
A report on facilities—present and future—needed to accommodate instructional television and other new educational programs. Prepared for EFL by Dave Chapman, Inc., Industrial Design.

THE SCHOOL LIBRARY
A report on facilities for independent study, with standards for the size of collections, seating capacity, and the nature of materials to be incorporated. (Geared to secondary schools, but much of the information is applicable to junior colleges.)

TO BUILD OR NOT TO BUILD
A study on the utilization of instructional space in small liberal arts colleges, with a do-it-yourself workbook for the individual use of those institutions that wish to survey their own utilization levels.

PROFILES OF SIGNIFICANT SCHOOLS

A series of reports which provide information on some of the latest developments in school planning and design. Profiles now available are...

> Belaire Elementary School, San Angelo, Texas
> Heathcote Elementary School, Scarsdale, New York
> Montrose Elementary School, Laredo, Texas
> Two Middle Schools, Saginaw Township, Michigan
> Newton South High School, Newton, Massachusetts
> Holland High School, Holland, Michigan

> Schools for Team Teaching—ten representative examples
> High Schools 1962: A Status Report on Educational Change and Architectural Consequence

CASE STUDIES OF EDUCATIONAL FACILITIES

A series of reports which provide information on specific solutions to problems in school planning, design, and construction. Now available...

1. CONVENTIONAL GYMNASIUM VS. GEODESIC FIELD HOUSE. West Bethesda High School, Montgomery County, Maryland.

2. SPACE AND DOLLARS: AN URBAN UNIVERSITY EXPANDS. A report on the economic physical expansion of urban universities based on a case study of the Drexel Institute of Technology.

3. LABORATORIES & CLASSROOMS FOR HIGH SCHOOL PHYSICS. Reprinted from MODERN PHYSICS BUILDINGS: DESIGN AND FUNCTION. A report of the American Association of Physics Teachers' and the American Institute of Physics' Project on Design of Physics Buildings.

4. A DIVISIBLE AUDITORIUM: BOULDER CITY, NEVADA. Case study of an auditorium that can be converted to instructional spaces by the use of soundproof, operable walls.

5. NEW CAMPUSES FOR OLD: A CASE STUDY OF FOUR COLLEGES THAT MOVED. What the decision to move means from an economic, academic, social, and physical point of view.

6. A COLLEGE HEALTH CENTER. Case study of a model center for small private colleges; architectural design by Caudill, Rowlett & Scott.